Even 1 from the Joe Zone

Seven Entertaining Short Stories

Joe B. Stallings, Jr.

outskirts
press

Even More Tales from the Joe Zone
Seven Entertaining Short Stories
All Rights Reserved.
Copyright © 2024 Joe B. Stallings, Jr.
v2.0

This is a work of fiction. Names, characters, businesses, places, events, locales, and incidents are either the products of the author's imagination or used in a fictitious manner. Any resemblance to actual persons, living or dead, or actual events is purely coincidental.

The opinions expressed in this manuscript are solely the opinions of the author and do not represent the opinions or thoughts of the publisher. The author has represented and warranted full ownership and/or legal right to publish all the materials in this book.

This book may not be reproduced, transmitted, or stored in whole or in part by any means, including graphic, electronic, or mechanical without the express written consent of the publisher except in the case of brief quotations embodied in critical articles and reviews.

Outskirts Press, Inc.
http://www.outskirtspress.com

ISBN: 978-1-9772-7122-8

Cover Photo © 2024 www.gettyimages.com. All rights reserved - used with permission.

Outskirts Press and the "OP" logo are trademarks belonging to Outskirts Press, Inc.

PRINTED IN THE UNITED STATES OF AMERICA

Contents

Introduction

I do break a few "rules" of writing.

One, don't use a big word when a simple word will do. I sometimes use archaic words. Why? Because when I read a story, I like to learn new words.

Two, don't leave things unexplained. I don't explain everything, as I think a person's imagination is part of the story.

Three, do not use facts in a fiction story. I like learning new things, so I throw in a fact here and there, but they fit and don't disrupt the story.

Four, yes, I use the word *that* occasionally when it isn't necessary. Sometimes it sounds better to me. Besides, if you diagram the sentence, you diagram *that* in the sentence even if it's not written.

When I use the word *blond*, I spell it without the letter e. *The Chicago Manual of Style* (*CMOS*) doesn't address using the word blond. The *CMOS* editors, however, like the position of *The Associated Press Stylebook*, which is that blond should be spelled without the e unless the word is being quoted.

I've already told you I like to use archaic words, but I can't promise that I always used them correctly. After all, we know how to use most words correctly because we have heard them spoken correctly, and we almost never hear archaic words. We say, "She is wearing a long yellow dress." We don't say, "She is wearing a yellow long dress." We say it correctly not because we know the grammar rule that an adjective of size comes before an adjective of color, but because we've heard it spoken that way.

I like em dashes, semicolons, and colons. Sometimes I go light with commas if they disrupt the flow of the sentence, which both introductory adverbs and introductory phrases do now and again. For example, if a character says, "Yes sir," I hear it as one word, so no comma. Also, you don't need a comma before a coordinating conjunction if it is connecting two short independent clauses. To me, an independent clause with five or fewer words is short, usually. Occasionally I don't care if the comma is there or not, so I may use one in this story and not the next. If a comma is missing, I almost certainly left it out on purpose.

I have no issues with using *they, them, their,* and *theirs* with a singular pronoun. Writers have been doing it for centuries, in part because there is no common-gender third-person singular pronoun. The refrain "Rewrite the sentence" is silly. I am amused by people who pitch a fit when *they* is used with a singular pronoun and then use *their* with a singular pronoun, completely unaware of the irony.

In one of my stories, I use a word I made up: *trailrod.* In that same story I use a word not in most dictionaries: Amis. That is German slang for Americans used after WWII, mainly in connection with American soldiers.

My stories are basically in order of how much I liked them and are meant to be entertaining and fun. It was truly enjoyable writing them.

1

The Cowboy from Where?

Western Territories United States—the 1870s

The cowboy on the horse stopped; there was a fork in the road. Two signs were nailed to a wooden post, one pointing this way, one pointing that way. Inscribed on one, *Blackberry*; inscribed on the other, *Places Not Blackberry*. The cowboy pulled a letter out of one of the raincoat pockets and glanced at the ending, "in the town of Blackberry, Western Territories." The letter was signed Kate Warne.

The cowboy's horse was packed with the usual cowboy supplies—a bedroll, a Winchester, saddlebags. A Colt pistol—clean, polished, shiny, and loaded—was hanging on the stranger's hip. Unofficially the stranger had been a cowboy for only three weeks. That's when the stranger arrived in St. Louis, bought supplies, and headed west. The prior twenty-four years had been spent back East.

An hour later, just after noon, the stranger entered Blackberry. It had been a tad windy and rainy, which accounted for the raincoat. The clouds were starting to drift away, and the sun was beginning to peek through. After tying up the horse, the stranger walked into the saloon.

The stranger perused the room. There were less than a dozen customers. Four well-dressed men were playing a friendly game of cards with toothpicks. A tall man who hadn't shaved for several days was leaning against the bar ordering a drink. In one corner a man sat alone with his head on the table—either sleeping or drunk—in any case not snoring. Three young women wearing traditional cotton dresses sat at a table discussing how to divide up the day's chores. Later they'd gussy up for their dancing and singing routine. At another table a single patron sat with a newspaper in front of his face. His? Most likely a man, as cigar smoke was floating up from behind the paper, the *Territorial Enterprise*. Kitty, the owner of the saloon, stood on the walkway one floor up, gazing over her domain. The walkway was lined with several doors to several rooms.

The stranger ambled to the bar and stared at the large painting that hung front and center. It wasn't exactly a painting. It was more of a sketch, a sketch done in pencil of a woman seated, her breasts partly visible, one more so than the other. Not so surprising, considering it was hanging in a saloon. But it was surprising—very surprising—inasmuch as it was a sketch of a woman breastfeeding her baby.

The bartender walked over to the stranger and asked, "What'll ya have?"

The stranger pointed to a bottle of whiskey on the shelf and held up one finger, meaning one shot.

"That's the expensive stuff," the bartender said.

The stranger took out a small coin and set it to spinning on the bar. Like most coins that go a-spinning, it attracted attention. Most of the folks watched or listened to the coin spinning until it finally came to a stop.

The bartender's eyes went wide. "A gold piece. You can have the whole bottle for that."

That comment got the attention of the whole kit and caboodle. Everybody gawked at the stranger now. The bartender poured the whiskey.

Unfortunately the patron at the bar closest to the stranger was a man named Gus. He did odd jobs for folks. And because he was also a gunslinger, he sometimes hired out as a problem solver. "Stranger, you should take your hat off in the saloon," Gus said. "Kitty might take offense. But tell ya what . . . share a shot of that whiskey with me, and all's forgiven."

Not bothering even to turn toward Gus, the stranger's head waggled left and right.

"You'll share that whiskey, or I'll call you out for a bit of gunplay in the street."

The stranger continued to ignore Gus.

"I'll be outside a-waitin' for ya. If you're not out in three minutes, I'll come back in and shoot ya. But first I'll shoot . . ." Gus looked around. "Vincent over there for good measure."

Vincent, the man sleeping or drunk, kept his head on the table.

Gus turned and stomped out of the saloon.

Yeah, trouble was expected in the Wild West, but this soon? The stranger walked over to Vincent, grabbed a handful of his hair, picked up his head, and looked at him. He was in no condition to abscond through the back door. The stranger sighed, gently lowered Vincent's head back onto the table, and moseyed out into the street.

The stranger lined up fourteen feet from Gus; pistols were inaccurate at longer distances, something the stranger knew but most gunslingers didn't. The stranger reached around and pulled the bottom of the raincoat to one side so as not to interfere with drawing the Colt.

Gus's arms hung by his side. The stranger took the same stance but appeared more relaxed. As a cross breeze blew, folks gathered to watch, mostly from inside the saloon or other buildings. Even the sheriff watched from inside his office.

As the tension built, someone down the street shouted, "The marshal is a-comin'!"

The hooves of a lone horse could be heard down the street getting closer.

Gus looked past the stranger and glimpsed the marshal. The stranger didn't turn around.

The marshal's horse passed to the left of the stranger. When the horse reached the midway point between the adversaries, it stopped. "You drunk, Gus?" the marshal asked.

"Nope."

"Y'all wait till I get inside the sheriff's office, then carry on." And the marshal rode on.

The stranger had never been in a gunfight but knew from extensive reading about the West that allowing yourself to be pushed around from the get-go meant you would be pretty much done for. The stranger's mind used the short interlude to hear the first movement from Beethoven's Fifth Symphony, to imagine the movement of the Colt, the aiming, and the pulling of the trigger.

The sheriff's office door opened, then closed.

A few seconds later Gus went for his pistol. As Gus's gun slid up from its holster, a bullet from the stranger's gun hit Gus's hand, and his gun fell to the ground.

Many of the citizens watching the gunfight were astounded. It happened so fast that no one—except the marshal, who had kept his eyes on the stranger's hand—even saw the stranger draw before the gun was back in its holster.

"Well, well," the marshal said aloud to himself, "never seen that before."

Gus wondered, should he fall to the ground, grab his pistol with his left hand, and shoot the stranger?

A gust of wind blew off the stranger's hat. It was hanging on the stranger's back, held on by a string around the neck.

The refrain, "What in tarnation," was heard.

Standing there displaying a head of short blond hair was a woman. A slight grin appeared on her face. Joey Storm Wilson—formerly or still, of Boston, Massachusetts—had just won her first gunfight. She had trained for this for twelve years. Joey was pleased with her reflexes, with her really hearing Beethoven's Fifth Symphony, with her inner calmness, and with her calculation of the crosswind's effect on the trajectory of the bullet.

Joey walked up to Gus, who stood bumfuzzled. She drew a whisky flask out of her raincoat pocket, removed the cork with her shiny white teeth, took Gus's injured hand, and poured some whiskey on it.

Gus pulled his hand away when the pain pinched his brain.

Joey put the cork back in the flask, took a cloth bandage roll from her raincoat pocket, reached over, and took Gus's hand again. She wrapped it with the bandage, ripping the end into two strips and then wrapping them back around and tying them together. "I wouldn't wait too long to have the doctor look at that," Joey said. She reached down, picked up Gus's pistol, and handed it to him. She started back to the saloon but turned to Gus and said, "Oh yeah, I'll be glad to let you have that drink now, but I'm not drinking with you. Not until your manners improve."

The crowd chuckled.

Joey continued to the saloon.

Gus said to himself, "Well dang, don't that beat a duck with a stick." He holstered his pistol and trudged to the saloon for his free drink.

"Barkeep!" Joey shouted, "give everyone a shot from my bottle."

The barkeep took the bottle and hurried around the room, giving everyone a glassful.

Joey took a table near Vincent, who was still out of it, and sat down.

Kitty appeared at Joey's table. "Mind if I join you?"

"Please."

"Never seen anything like you in these parts. What's your name?"

"Joey S. Wilson."

"S?"

"Storm."

"Appropriate name for someone dauntless."

"My mother insisted on the name."

"Oh?"

"I was born during a hurricane while high winds and heavy rains lashed the house. Doctor couldn't get there. Between the piercing screams of joy—as my mother described it later—she shouted out instructions to my father, who, bless his heart, didn't faint until it was all over."

"Where was this?"

"Boston."

"Boston. You from Boston?"

"Yes. Lived there my whole life—up until several weeks ago."

"Imagine that . . . a *cowboy from where* . . . Boston, and you can shoot like that?"

"When I was twelve, I read a book about the West and it

became an obsession, after a fashion. I started shooting pistols and rifles and riding horses almost every day.

"You got the shooting down pat—that's for sure. I've never seen anyone hit Gus before his gun was out of the holster. Were you aiming to hit his hand?"

Joey smiled.

"Sakes alive!"

"Where's the best place to stay in town?"

"We're not officially a hotel, but I do have a few rooms to rent out now and again for folks I'm partial to. Of course, it can get loud."

"You have any other guests?"

"Two. Vincent over there; he's a foreigner. From Europe I think. He helps out around the place, cleaning and other odds and ends. He drew that sketch that's hanging behind the bar. When he got to town he seemed a bit out of sorts. I felt sorry for him, so I hired him. And Samuel over there reading the newspaper. He's quite a character. People sit around his table just to listen to his stories for hours. He's very entertaining. Want me to introduce you?"

"Maybe later."

The marshal stepped into the saloon and cozied up to the bar, close enough to hear Joey and Kitty's conversation.

"What in the world is Joey Storm Wilson from Boston doing in Blackberry—the middle of nowhere?" Kitty asked.

Joey hadn't figured she'd need to explain; she quickly came up with an answer that seemed plausible. "I wanted to see what the West was really like. And I think a friend of mine, Kate Warne, is here. I got a letter from her a few weeks ago."

"Kate Warne, Kate Warne. Oh yeah. But she left a few days ago. I didn't talk with her much. She must have enjoyed Samuel's stories, as she was often at his table."

"That's disappointing that I missed her. But I'll stay a few days and rest up until I decide where to head next."

"Fine. A room is three bits a night. That includes breakfast whenever you get up. You want the room?"

"Sure."

"I need to get back to business. I'll talk with you later."

After Kitty walked away, the marshal came over to Joey's table. He pulled out a chair, turned it backward, sat down facing Joey, and pushed the front of his hat up just a tad. "Mind if I have a seat?"

"It looks like you already have, Marshal."

"I was watching your hand when you drew."

"Yeah."

"Never seen anyone draw like that."

"My own special method. Fastest way I could find to draw. Been practicing it a long time."

"I believe it. No one will beat you with that draw. Maybe I'll start drawin' that way myself."

"It takes a lot of practice—a lot—to get it right. And even longer if you're in the habit of drawing the usual way. By the time you get it down, it'd be time to retire."

"You're probably right. How many gunslingers could you take without getting hit?"

"Four normally. Six or seven if I'm wearing a Colt on both hips. I've tested it . . . using blanks, of course."

"Would your aim be as accurate as it was with Gus? Assuming you were aiming for his hand."

"As accurate, no. But I'd still hit the person unless they were moving around or lying on the ground—smaller target."

"You aiming for more gunfights while you're here?"

"No, don't think most men will want to get into a gunfight with a woman. The chivalry thing."

"Why didn't you take your hat off beforehand to avoid the gunfight if being a woman would have prevented it?"

"I knew I wouldn't have to hurt him much and wanted people to know how quick I am. Hope that combination, fast draw and being a woman, will keep me out of gunfights."

"I hope you're right. See ya around." At that the marshal stood, tipped his hat, and ambled out of the saloon.

Vincent was beginning to stir.

Joey walked over to the bartender.

"You have any coffee?"

"Sure do, Miss."

"Can you bring two cups to Vincent's table?"

"Sure thing."

"Thanks."

Joey headed to Vincent's table, pulled out a chair, and sat. Vincent was sitting upright, looking around. The bartender delivered two cups of coffee.

"Good afternoon, Vincent. My name's Joey."

Vincent drank some of his coffee.

"Afternoon . . . oh . . . I see. Good afternoon. Don't recall you."

"Just got into town. I'm from Boston."

"Boston. That's where I arrived when I got to this country."

"From where?"

"My ship sailed from London. Needed to get away."

"You got away all right—far away. What were you doing in London?"

"I was working at Goupil & Cie."

"Ah, the auction house."

Vincent looked at Joey with an inquisitive face.

"No one within a thousand miles of this godforsaken place would know Goupil & Cie. How is it you do?"

"Like I said, I'm from Boston. I've been to their gallery in New York City. My parents bought a few things from them."

Vincent leaned to his right to look at his new friend's attire, both over and under the table.

"You're dressed like a cowboy; you're wearing a pistol."

"America's a funny place, Vincent. I'm sure you've realized that by now."

"Funny's not a word I'd use. Primitive and unsettled, I'd say."

"You miss it? Europe? The gaiety, the civility, your family? Tell me about the wonderful things there. I've been wanting to go."

Before he knew it, Vincent had spent two hours talking about Europe. Now and again a little tear journeyed down his face. He missed it; that much was clear.

The next morning Joey got dressed, put on her holster, and parked the Colt on her hip. Then she headed down to breakfast. She saw Samuel reading his paper and walked over to his table.

"Mind if I join you?" Joey asked.

"Certainly not, young lady."

"What are you doing here?"

"Me? Just passing through on my way back East."

"Just passing through? I doubt that. Does anyone here know we're friends?"

"I haven't told a soul."

"Did Dad send you?"

"It certainly wasn't your mother. She doesn't suffer fools gladly. And she has complete confidence in you and your abilities. I still remember the look on your father's face when he discovered that your mother had bought you a Colt and a Winchester five years earlier when you were only twelve. I don't know that he understood your mother until that day when he realized that she treated you not just as female, but as a person. Your mother certainly is assiduous in all that she does."

"So, have you reported in?"

"To your dad—a telegram yesterday. Didn't give him any details. Said you were fine and staying out of trouble. Now your mother, that's different. No sugarcoating in her telegram. Bet she was radiant all day—probably will be all week."

"I understand Kate Warne enjoyed your stories while she was here."

"My stories? Just the opposite. Does she have some tales to tell. You know she's the one who discovered the plot to assassinate Abraham Lincoln in 1860 when he was on the way to Washington for the inauguration? And she was involved in the obfuscation to get him to Washington safely. Thank God she convinced Allan Pinkerton to hire her as a full-time detective in 1856, or history might be different. First woman detective ever."

"Glad you enjoyed her company. Mom always invites her to stay with us when she's in Boston."

"Was she in Blackberry doing something for you?"

"What makes you ask that?"

"Well . . . she was here . . . now you're here."

"Happenstance methinks." The corners of Joey's mouth went up a tad.

"Oh, that reminds me. I've got a letter for you from your brother. I met up with him at Fort Carson on the way here." Samuel slid an envelope across the table.

Joey opened it, read it, and lit a match; the letter burned to a crisp.

"When are you leaving Blackberry?" Joey asked Samuel.

"On the three o'clock stage."

"I'd like you to do me a favor."

"Name it."

"Buy the sketch behind the bar. It belongs to Vincent, and I'm sure Kitty won't mind. I believe Vincent's going to be needing some cash. I'll give you the money. Take the sketch with you when you leave town." Then Joey explained what Samuel was to do with the sketch.

"Oh," Samuel said. "I've been meaning to ask you about the Medieval Days Fair they held in Boston a few months back."

"Yeah?"

"Didn't you enter the jousting tournament?"

"Yes."

"How'd you do? Weren't you supposed to joust that big man Randolph Stonewood? I understand he's tall and handsome."

"I did joust Mr. Stonewood. But considering I only had one week of practice, and he's been jousting at the fairs for years, how do you think I did?"

"That bad?"

"In no time at all I was lying flat on my back on the hard ground wearing a hundred pounds of armor, with a stout Mr. Stonewood standing over me."

Samuel chuckled slightly. "So why did you do it?"

"Maybe I was trying to impress him, or maybe I just like a challenge."

"Did you . . . impress him?"

"Not like I hoped. After all, if I had to be flat on my back at the hands of Mr. Randolph Stonewood, I would have preferred to be on a bed wearing something silky."

Samuel burst out laughing. Anyone in town still sleeping wasn't after that explosion.

"Young lady, I'm glad your father wasn't here to hear you say that. But I'm certainly glad I was." Samuel laughed some more. "Once you're home I want to hear all about your trip," Samuel said with a look of glee. "No doubt it'll be quite a tale."

Joey got up.

"You going somewhere?" Samuel asked.

"Yes, got a few things to do. Here's the money for the sketch. Make sure it's boxed up but *good*."

"Using *good* as an adverb, you know some people don't take kindly to that."

"Why do you think I do it. I'll see you at the stage office before you leave."

"Fine, fine, young lady. See you there. I'll just wink; keep people from knowing we're friends."

Joey walked down to Fay's Boardinghouse on the edge of town and entered the dining room. When she heard noises from the kitchen, she headed there and found a woman zipping around nonstop.

"Excuse me . . . you Fay?" Joey asked.

"Why, Miss Wilson, yes I am, and I must say I'm most pleased to make your acquaintance." Fay gave Joey a firm handshake. "Can't tell ya the tingles I got seeing a woman outshoot a man. Goodness me, never thought I'd see such a thing."

"Glad you enjoyed it. I've practiced a lot."

"No doubt about that, child, no doubt. What can I do for ya?"

"Do you have a room available?"

"Aren't you staying at the saloon?"

"It's a bit noisy for me. Besides, I plan on staying a week or so and need a place that offers three meals a day."

"Have a couple of rooms available. You can take your pick of the litter."

They went upstairs to pick out a room.

"This is the best room. Thought you should see it first."

Joey sat down on the bed and bounced up and down a time or two. "Do all your rooms have beds made by the Wilson company?"

"Yep, sure do. They're the best-made beds in the country. Wouldn't use anything else."

"Me either. I've slept on Wilson's virtually my whole life. Had to since my father is one of the company founders and the vice president."

Fay chuckled. "You telling me your father is Henry Wilson?" Fay stared at Joey who just smiled. "A laud have mercy," Fay said as she dropped onto the bed too. "Can't believe it; just can't believe it. Still have to charge you for the room."

"As well you should."

After all the particulars were worked out, Joey had one more request.

"You want the table where?" Fay asked, thinking she had misunderstood.

"Outside. And I expect to have a guest for dinner today. It will be a long dinner, and I want to get started around five."

"Okay. You certainly are full of surprises, young lady. You planning on having a guest for all your meals?"

"No, not usually." Joey pulled some money out of her pocket and gave it to Fay.

Joey showed up at the stagecoach office a few minutes before the stage pulled out. As promised, Samuel gave her a wink. The sketch had been boxed up and loaded onto the stage.

After the stage pulled away amidst a cloud of dust, Joey returned to her room at Fay's. Around four thirty she headed downstairs wearing quite the gown. Even a blind man in a dust storm couldn't mistake her for a man now. She looked dressed for the opera; and with such radiance, you would think you were in another world. She headed down the street to pick up Vincent for dinner. There wasn't a single person—neither man nor woman—who didn't crane their neck to watch Joey pass by.

Not long after, Joey and Vincent sat at the table that had been placed outside Fay's, waiting for their supper.

"This remind you of an outdoor café in Paris?" Joey asked.

Vincent looked around and started to snicker but thought better of it.

"Well, it's missing some . . . other tables . . . ambience."

They both laughed. Then they talked and talked and talked. While they were eating, the talking slowed down, but not much. Though Vincent talked the most, Joey piped in now and again.

"You know what I want to do someday, Vincent?"

"What?"

"I want to spend a week or two in Vienna. I want to waltz nonstop at a Johann Strauss concert."

"Ah, the Waltz King. He's certainly all the rage in Vienna these days."

That thought got Vincent going on apropos the music scene in Europe. Before they knew it, darkness had enveloped them, and bookoodles of stars were out.

"I have something to tell you, Joey."

"Yes?"

"I've decided to go home, back to Europe. Samuel bought my sketch, and now I've got enough money for the trip. America's just not for me. I bought a ticket for tomorrow's stage."

"Good for you, Vincent. I'm happy for you and wish you the best."

"Thank you."

"It's been a long day; I think I'll turn in."

"Okay. I'll sit here a bit and enjoy the starry night."

"Well, goodnight."

The next day Joey was at the stagecoach office to say good-bye and wish Vincent good luck. Then she went to the saloon for a drink.

Joey sat at a table with her drink.

"May I join you?" Kitty asked.

"Sure."

"If you're going to be hanging around a bit longer, I've got something to warn you about."

"Is that so?"

"Yes, Hendon Kneece. He's president of the local bank. He may invite you to lunch, and he almost certainly will want to show you his vault."

"His vault?"

"Yeah, the bank vault. He's real proud of it and likes to show it off to people he thinks are classy. It boosts his sense of importance, although he's somewhat of a nitwit. But it really is a bigger, stronger vault than a town of this size needs. Big as a bedroom it is. Mr. Crawford is probably subsidizing the bank. Mr. Crawford's the biggest rancher around here; he pretty much gets what he wants."

"That's interesting."

"Isn't it though."

"Has he shown you the vault?"

"Yes, and there is something interesting in it."

"Oh."

"In one corner is a stack of something covered up with a large tablecloth. Most of us who've seen it think it's empty boxes and that Hendon is just trying to be mysterious. But if you have a chance, you might want to take a look. Considering your wide-ranging abilities, you might be able to wangle it. Who knows? With you being Henry Wilson's daughter, maybe he'll show you what's under the tablecloth."

Joey had figured it wouldn't take long for it to get around town that she was Henry Wilson's daughter. At least among those folks who knew who Henry Wilson was, that is.

"I'll keep that in mind."

"See you later."

The next morning Joey, dressed in her cowboy duds with her Colt on her hip, then went downstairs for breakfast.

"Good morning, Miss Wilson," Fay said.

"Good morning."

As Joey took her seat, Fay had breakfast in front of her in no time.

"You got a visitor rocking on the front porch, Miss Wilson," Fay said after she put out the breakfast.

"Oh."

"Yep, Mr. Hendon Kneece. I can guess what he wants to show ya."

"Me too, Fay. I've been warned."

After breakfast Joey moved onto the porch.

"Oh, good morning, Miss Wilson," Mr. Kneece said as he stood up from the rocking chair.

"Good morning to you too. Mr. Kneece, I believe?"

"Yes ma'am. President of the town's only bank. And quite a bank we've got too."

"Is that so?"

"Yes sirree. I think you'd be most impressed. It's not much compared to the bank your father uses in Boston, I'm sure, but it's got the biggest vault in the Western Territories. Perhaps you'd like a personal tour?"

"That would be lovely."

"Great. I'm heading to the bank now. If that's convenient for you of course."

"Yes indeed."

A few minutes later they were inside the bank lobby as Mr. Kneece recited the bank's history. Joey couldn't see the vault from the lobby. Twenty minutes later Mr. Kneece lit a kerosene lamp, and they walked through a wide hallway, past some heavy curtains, and to the door of the vault.

"Miss Wilson, no visit to the bank would be complete without a tour of the vault."

Mr. Kneece put down the kerosene lamp, turned the dial of the vault a few times, and opened it.

"If you'll follow me, Miss Wilson."

They both entered the vault, and Mr. Kneece spent a few minutes on its history.

"Miss Wilson, if I may draw your attention to the back right corner."

"Why it looks like a tablecloth on a bunch of boxes. I don't suppose you eat lunch on it?"

Mr. Kneece laughed.

"No. No, I don't. But I've got a treat for you, Miss Wilson. I've never shown anyone what's under the tablecloth and behind the empty boxes in the front there, but you, being the daughter of Henry Wilson, I'm sure there's no danger."

Mr. Kneece moved to the back right corner and motioned for Joey to follow. He carefully set down the kerosene lamp, pulled off the tablecloth, and moved the empty boxes.

"Never seen anything like that have you?"

"I should say not, Mr. Kneece. That has to be what—two million worth of gold bars?"

"Two and a half million, Miss Wilson."

"I didn't realize you were so well-off."

"Oh, it's not mine. No. It belongs to Mr. Crawford. He made it back East during the Civil War. The government was spending money right and left then. Here, hold one of the bars."

Joey took the gold bar from Mr. Kneece, ran her fingers along the top, and turned the bar over. The letters "WV" and some numbers were etched into it.

"I'm most impressed, Mr. Kneece. Who all knows this gold is here?"

"Almost no one. You're the first person I've shown it to who doesn't work for Mr. Crawford."

"I see."

"Of course, Miss Wilson, we don't want anyone else to know."

"I understand."

Joey set the gold bar down, and Mr. Kneece put the empty boxes and tablecloth back in place. After they finished in the vault, Mr. Kneece walked Miss Wilson to the bank entrance and bid her good day.

Then Joey took a roundabout route to the telegraph office. She walked up to the telegraph window.

"I want to send a telegram," she told the clerk as casually as if she had been reporting the weather.

"Certainly," the telegraph operator said, and he pulled out a piece of paper and a pencil.

Then the pair just stood and stared at each other.

Joey pulled out a gold coin, put it on the ledge, and said again in a stronger voice, "I need to send a telegram."

"Yes ma'am, and I'm ready to take a telegram."

"You don't understand. I . . . myself . . . need to send the telegram. I know Morse code."

"Can't let ya do that," the operator said. "I could get into a lot of trouble."

Joey pulled out a couple more gold coins, showed them to the operator, and tossed them into his office. They bounced all over kingdom come, hitting the floor, the walls, and the tables . . .

"Oh, would you look at that," Joey said. "How clumsy of me. I'll come in and pick them up. It'll only take me a moment. Maybe you can go in the back and take inventory while I'm looking for them. But I bet I won't be able to find a-one."

"Come to think of it, I do need to do this month's inventory."

The operator got up, unlocked his front door so Joey could enter, and headed for the back room. Joey walked in, sat down, and started sending the telegram. Meanwhile, the operator shuffled a few things around in the back before moving as close as he dared to listen. He missed who the telegram was sent to, but he heard and deciphered the rest of the dots and dashes.

The tallest tale we were told by our godfather is true. It's here. I will need help.

Joey

Earlier, Mr. Crawford's foreman, Butler Sooner, had gone to the bank to make a deposit when he saw Mr. Kneece and Joey. He saw Mr. Kneece invite Joey into the vault. He made his deposit and headed back to the ranch.

"Hendon knows not to show anyone the gold," Mr. Crawford said.

"Yeah," Butler replied, "but we know he's taken people inside the vault before."

"But never showed the gold. Who was the person?"

"I don't know her name."

"Her?"

"Yeah. It's the woman who outdrew Gus."

"My, my, the female gunslinger."

"Okay. You go back into town and find out if she sent any telegrams. I'll go to the marshal's office and see what I can find out about this woman. We'll meet up at the saloon.

Butler walked up to the telegraph office window.

"Bert, you send any telegrams this morning?"

"Telegrams . . . for anyone in particular?"

"That female gunslinger."

"God's truth, I can say I did not send any telegrams for Miss Wilson."

"Thanks, Bert. If you do, Mr. Crawford would like to know."

"Sure thing."

Butler hurried away, and Bert was glad as he was sweating profusely. At the same time, Mr. Crawford stopped in to pay the marshal a visit.

"Mr. Crawford. What can I do for you?"

"This new female in town—the one that outdrew Gus."

"Yeah, what about her?"

"Who is she?"

"Joey Wilson. And Mr. Crawford, I'd suggest that you and anyone else not get into a shooting match with her."

"Oh?"

"She'll outdraw anyone. I guarantee it."

"Marshal, that seems a bit of a stretch."

"I saw her draw against Gus. She doesn't draw like a regular cowboy. She doesn't take the Colt out of the holster. Once her hand is on the gun, she tilts it, holster and all, and pulls the trigger. No pulling the gun out of the holster, no bringing up the gun to aim."

Mr. Crawford's eyes narrowed as he stared at the marshal.

"You couldn't hit the side of a barn shooting like that."

"Maybe not, but she can. She was aiming for Gus's hand, and it was movin', but she hit it anyway. Never seen nothin' like it."

"Thanks, Marshal," Mr. Crawford said before he headed to the saloon.

The marshal realized he forgot to mention that Joey was Henry Wilson's daughter.

Mr. Crawford and Butler had been at a table talking for a while. Mr. Crawford waved Suzy over; she was one of Kitty's girls.

"Yes, Mr. Crawford, anything else I can get you?"

"Yeah, Suzy. Your brother Jeffers. He still in Amarillo hiring out his gun?"

"Yes, Mr. Crawford, he is. That's why I'm here. I don't like seein' him do that kind of work."

"He still staying at the Mackave Hotel?"

"Far as I know, Mr. Crawford."

"Thanks, Suzy. Maybe a couple more drinks."

"Sure thing," she said, and she hurried off to get the drinks.

"Butler, I'll meet you back at the ranch. But first I want you to send a telegram. Let me write it out.

Amarillo
Mackave Hotel
Jeffers Smith

Need you and eleven other men in Blackberry quickly. Problem needs handling. Double your normal fee.

Crawford

The next day Jeffers and five of his men were at the Crawford ranch.

"Five? You only brought *five* other gunslingers with you? I said eleven!" Mr. Crawford shouted.

"One person—and a woman at that. We won't have any problem."

"You idiot. She hit Gus's hand before he could even get his gun out of the holster. Her draw is quicker than anyone the marshal's ever seen. And let me tell you something else. You know who raised me?"

"No sir," Jeffers said, wondering what that had to do with anything.

"My aunts. I was raised by three women. And I can tell

you; men always underestimate women—always. I've seen it time and again."

"So what do you want me to do?"

"Take six of my ranch hands with you. That's the only way you'll have a chance."

In the West it was never hard to get into a gunfight. You just threaten to shoot someone else, like Gus had, if the person didn't meet you outside.

Joey was standing in the middle of the street in front of the saloon. Down the street were the gunslingers hired by Mr. Crawford—twelve of them. Not exactly the best odds for Joey. Sure, because of her quick draw she could get several of them before they got her, but certainly not all twelve.

At that moment Suzy, Jeffers's sister, ran into the street and up to Jeffers.

"Jeffers, you have to stop this," Suzy said. "Turn around and walk away."

"None of your concern. Get on . . . outta the way," Jeffers said, pushing Suzy in the direction of the saloon.

"Her father is Henry Wilson."

"The vice president of the Wilson Mattress Company? So!"

"No, you idiot! The vice president of the United States . . . *the United States*. Her godfather is Ulysses S. Grant for God's sake. Uncle Ulysses, she calls him."

Jeffers paused, looked at Suzy, and burst out laughing. "Uh-huh, and you're the queen of England, and I'm the chancellor of the exchequer."

"Huh?" Exasperated, Suzy raced back to the saloon.

"My, my, Joey. You been tellin' some tall tales," Jeffers shouted out. "Gotta give ya credit for creativity though. But next time come up with something more believable. I suppose the bartender is your brother?"

"Could be, but he's not. Jim Wilson is my brother."

"I'd like to meet your brother."

"I can arrange that."

"A shame you're not gonna have the chance."

"Oh, I don't know. He's a major in the US Cavalry. No tellin' where he might be."

At that exact moment the cotton canvas covering on the two Western wagons—one to her left and one to her right—slid onto the ground.

"How you doing, big brother?" Joey asked without taking her eyes off of Jeffers.

Jim was standing in one wagon with two cavalrymen. Two more cavalrymen were in the other wagon. The odds had changed . . . six to twelve now. Changed all right, but certainly more lopsided than that. In both wagons a cavalry officer was sitting behind a Gatling gun, ready to fire 400 rounds a minute.

"Fine, little sister. Uncle Ulysses says thanks for finding the gold that was stolen while it was on its way to Philadelphia from the West Virginia mint during the Civil War. Mom wants to know what's with the sketch of the woman breastfeeding her baby that Samuel—I mean Mark Twain—dropped off at the house. And Dad wants to know if you're coming home now that you got Vincent to go back home to Europe like you promised his brother Theo Van Gogh you would."

Twelve unbuckled gun belts hit the ground.

The End

2

I Think I Would, Sugar

Captain John "Johnny" Meredith was driving the jeep on a narrow out-of-the-way road through mostly forest, with a farm here and there, in Southern Germany—in the American Occupation Zone. As a rule, one of the three enlisted soldiers in the jeep should have been driving, but Captain Meredith knew the way—they didn't. It was May 28, 1945, several weeks after Germany's surrender. Johnny had been visiting another Army command and was ordered to take the three soldiers to his base of operations—a transfer. Germany lay in ruins, and there were more than three million US soldiers in the country.

Captain Meredith had joined the Army five years prior—a year before the US entered World War II. Being the student of history that he was, he foresaw the United States joining the fight and wanted to be in the Army ready to go when it happened. His parents were disappointed but not surprised that he had joined right after graduating with a degree in journalism. He had a keen sense of history and felt that being a soldier would be helpful in writing about the war later.

As the men in the jeep rode, they could see a young boy standing in the middle of the road up ahead waving a stick

with a white cloth tied to it. The sergeant, sitting in the pas-
senger's seat, started to pick up the rifle lying across his lap.

"Gentlemen," Johnny said, "weapons will not be necessary."

The jeep slowed and came to a stop several yards in front
of the boy.

"Toll road, one pack of cigarettes and one bag of coffee,
please," the young boy said.

"A bag of coffee *and* a pack of cigarettes? This isn't exactly
the autobahn to Berlin," Johnny said.

"Okay. For you—today only—a pack of cigarettes," the boy
said with a smile.

Johnny reached into his pocket, pulled out an unopened
pack, and handed it to the boy. With all the shortages, both
cigarettes and coffee were a form of money.

At that moment they heard someone shouting off to the
left. A young woman ran across the field toward them.

"Hans, stop that, you silly boy," the woman shouted.

The enlisted men started reaching for their weapons.

"At ease, men, at ease," Johnny said forcefully.

The woman had almost reached the jeep.

"Hans, how many times . . . Oh! . . . Captain Meredith,
I'm sorry, I didn't realize it was you." She looked at the boy.
"Hans, how many times have Mom and Dad told you not to
collect tolls?" Lorelei admonished.

Hans shrugged and started across the field as Lorelei
watched. She turned back to the soldiers.

"Johnny, I . . ." she caught herself and glanced at the other
three soldiers. "I mean, Captain Meredith, I wish you wouldn't
encourage him."

The enlisted men glanced at each other with a questioning
gaze after Lorelei said "Johnny."

Lorelei's face was brimming with delight.

"Are you coming to supper this Saturday as usual, Captain Meredith?"

"Of course. Your parents doing okay?"

"Yes sir, Captain Meredith."

"Lorelei, it's quite okay to call me Johnny. That's my name."

"Yes sir, I mean . . . of course . . . Johnny."

Lorelei gazed into Captain Meredith's eyes before she turned and started back across the field to her parents' farmhouse, twisting her dress to and fro as she skipped like a teenager. She was twenty-eight but had told Captain Meredith that she was twenty. She lied to Captain Meredith on occasion—but only when it was absolutely necessary.

The jeep started, and the four US soldiers were on their way again.

"Captain," the sergeant said, "you do know that the three of us are military police?"

"Sergeant, considering you've got MP plastered on your uniforms, armbands, and helmets, I'd have to be woolgathering not to."

"You realize that once we get to the base, sir, we're going to have to take you into custody for fraternization. I mean, sir, you are aware that US soldiers are not allowed to talk to German civilians. And Captain, it's pretty clear you've been doing that—and more."

"Sergeant, let me be candid. First, that boy Hans works for Colonel Gaskins as a German interpreter, so I have to talk to him on occasion and so will you. He's sort of in the Army too. Second, do you know what the OSS is?"

"Isn't that the Office of Strategic Services, sir? They handle spies and covert operations."

"That's right, Sergeant. Colonel Gaskins is big on helping

the OSS. I seriously think he is one of them; but that's just me. Our Army unit helps the OSS quite a bit, certainly more often than other units do. The OSS believes there are some high-level Nazis roaming around Southern Germany. Lorelei Bauer and her parents are farmers, and with the food shortage, they are very popular. They hear a lot of gossip. I eat supper with them several times a week, and I pass the gossip on to Colonel Gaskins. A few other officers under his command, like me, speak, read, and write German, and they're doing the same thing. So even if General Eisenhower were around, I suggest you tread lightly with enforcing the fraternization policy as the colonel was in high school with President Truman, and the colonel doesn't suffer fools gladly. I suggest you review the policy with him so you know what's what."

"Yes sir. Thank you, sir. I'll do that."

Captain Meredith was in his office with the door open. The building was in an area commandeered by Colonel Gaskins as a base of operations. It included an assortment of other build-ings in a small town in Germany not too far from Munich. The small town was chosen as a base of operations as it hadn't been bombed to smithereens like most of the larger cities in Germany. It was after work hours, and Captain Meredith was typing one letter to his parents and one to his wife.

Dear Mom and Dad,

I'm sure by the time you get this letter you will know that the war is over—at least with Germany. I'm sure y'all are relieved that the fighting is over and that

I am out of harm's way. I will be doing administrative work mostly. Since I know German, I will be reading a lot of files and interviewing Germans.

We are operating under a no-fraternization policy with the Germans. Technically we're not even allowed to speak with them. The biggest problem with that policy—and there are many problems—is all the children that run up to us here and there and want candy and other goodies. I've heard that the rule doesn't apply to children under twelve, but we're waiting for confirmation. Of course that doesn't apply to me if I'm working in my official capacity of getting information from the Germans. Also, since I have a journalism degree, I have been asked to write articles now and again for the military newspaper. And with a journalist ID, I have carte blanche to fraternize with Germans.

Even with all the pictures and articles y'all will see of Germany, you can't begin to appreciate the true plight of the Europeans. That's all for now.

Love, Johnny

Dearest Clarissa,

I'm sure you're overjoyed that the war is over. At the same time, I'm sure it's giving you some trepidation. Mayhap trepidation is too strong; how about butterflies? I'm sure we're like thousands of other couples who got married after knowing each other for a short time because of the war. Sure, we only knew each other for two weeks and haven't seen each other in three years. But those two weeks in the hustle and bustle of Washington on a war footing were magical.

Things here are in chaos. I am glad that you lived out the war in Des Moines far from any danger. I assume your sister is still working for the War Department. I'm sure glad you were in DC to visit her three years ago, or we would have never met.

I won't be coming home soon, especially since I know German. Perhaps once things settle down here, you can visit me.

Love,
Johnny

It was Saturday night, and Captain Meredith was at the table with the Bauer family. He had brought some of the food that Frau Bauer had prepared. He also gave them a few bags of coffee. It was the least he could do.

"What's the latest gossip?" Johnny asked no one in particular.

"Well," Herr Bauer said, "some high-level Nazi is around, but I haven't heard any name. I'll skip the gossip concerning the black market. We all realize that the Amis don't have enough men to even begin enforcing the laws against it. Unfortunately it is a necessary evil in these times."

"I know," Johnny replied. "Things on the farm okay?"

"Papa, what about the tractor?" Hans interjected.

"Now, that's nothing to bother Captain Meredith with."

"What about the tractor?"

"It broke down yesterday. I can fix the little things. But this . . ." Herr Bauer shrugged his shoulders.

"Wednesday I'll bring a mechanic with me. I'll come a little early so he can look over the tractor. As a reward, maybe he can join us for supper."

"That would be most appreciated," Herr Bauer replied with resignation.

There was a knock at the door. Everyone froze. An unexpected visitor was never a good thing in these lawless times. Herr Bauer got up and headed to the door. Johnny followed but stayed back a bit. He put his hand on the pistol handle in his holster.

Herr Bauer opened the door.

"Bert," Herr Bauer said, "what are you doing here?"

Bert walked into the house.

"Is that any way to treat your brother?"

"Of course, welcome, welcome. It's just you rarely visit—and out of the blue."

Johnny turned and tiptoed back to the table, unsure if Herr Bauer wanted his brother to see him.

Herr Bauer didn't care and brought Bert into the dining room. Bert stopped when he saw Johnny in an Amis uniform.

"Bert, this is Captain Meredith. He was running off some thieves nearby, and we invited him for supper." Herr Bauer felt it best to make up a story.

"Ah," Bert said, seemingly oblivious to the fact that Johnny was an American officer. Looking at the table, Bert said, "I haven't had supper and—"

"Please, have a seat," Herr Bauer said.

The dinner conversation completely stopped for five, ten minutes, and then Bert asked, "Lorelei, why aren't you in your uniform?"

Frau Bauer dropped her fork on her plate, creating a loud clanking noise. The contrast with the prior silence was deafening. Everyone stopped and looked at Lorelei; tension filled the room.

After five or six seconds of awkward silence:

"Uncle, you're confusing me with someone else."

"Oh," Bert said as he looked over at Johnny. "Yes, I guess so."

Breathing restarted, as did eating. Everyone was hushed for a few more minutes.

"She's coming . . . Marlene," Bert said.

"Then perhaps it's best you go home. You don't want to miss her," Herr Bauer said.

"Oh, yes . . . yes I should."

Bert stood up and Herr Bauer walked him to the door and said goodbye. Then he returned to the table and sat down.

"Sorry, Captain Meredith. My brother is odd sometimes— well, often actually. I don't think he even realized you were an Amis. His Marlene is Marlene Dietrich. He saw a picture of her fifteen, twenty years ago and fell in love. He has been convinced ever since that she is on her way here to marry him. Says it can't be any other way; since he's in love, she must be too. Bert and his crazy thoughts. He's always writing her letters."

It was lunchtime and Johnny was in his office with the door open. He had just received a letter from Clarissa. He read it, then wrote his parents and Clarissa.

Ever Dearest Johnny,

Butterflies, absolutely. How could it be otherwise? After we were married in the lobby of the hotel where you were staying, you had to scoot to catch your train. After being married for three years, I imagine few married couples can claim they have not consummated their marriage. But alas, desperate times. I hope you are not regretting your decision. This, however, isn't a topic that can be adequately thrashed out in letters. Hopefully I can see you soon.

Oh, I've been meaning to tell you, Mom and Dad have had some German POWs working on the farm.

Love,
Clarissa

Dear Mom and Dad,

I'm glad to hear that the war with Japan is over too. You can't even begin to understand the turmoil here in Germany—and all of Europe for that matter. There are millions upon millions of displaced people; slave laborers working in German factories trying to get back to whatever county they were taken from; Jews trying to get to their former homes, the West, or Israel; German soldiers trying to get home; Eastern Europeans trying to leave countries controlled by the Russians; and millions of others, displaced for millions of reasons. The UN is running camps for displaced persons, but they can't even begin to help them all. And there is simply not enough food to feed everyone. Thousands will starve—even with our help.

Love for now,
Johnny

Dearest Clarissa,

I wasn't surprised to hear that your parents are using German POWs on the farm. Other allies are doing that too, using POWs for manual labor. But of course we are treating the POWs humanely, unlike the Russians.

As you can imagine, US soldiers are chomping at the bit to get home. But with so many US ships in the Pacific, it is slow going. Soon I expect the Army will start allowing visitors from the US. I'll keep you posted.

Love,
Johnny

"Hans," Bertha said, "I'm going to need a couple of packs of cigarettes to get us food."

"Here you go. I'm expecting to get a carton later today from Captain Meredith."

"Don't tell me that you went ahead with your harebrained scheme to sell all the original Nazi party membership cards to the Amis?"

"Yes I have."

"But you don't have them. You don't even have a clue if they exist anymore."

"The Amis don't know that. And if my plan works, we may end up with a couple of boxes of cigarettes. Boxes, Bertha; imagine that. And the Amis have bigger fish to fry than some short, round, bald German man. And with the food shortage, they're not going to lock me up—that's just another mouth to feed."

"This war was so foolish. Rationing almost from day one. And I told you, I told you it would get worse as the war continued. You're not so round anymore, not with ration cards that have allowed us only 1,000 calories a day over the past year."

Bertha kissed Hans on the forehead and patted what belly he did have. Then she left their bombed-out apartment with no running water, no electricity, and no phone, in search of food.

"Lieutenant Shepard," Captain Meredith called out after he pulled up to the motor pool.

"Yes sir?"

"I need to borrow one of your mechanics for several hours. It involves an assignment off base for Colonel Gaskins. I won't have the mechanic back until late. It'll help if he's a farm boy and has worked on tractors."

"Yes sir. I know just the soldier."

"Fine. I need him right away. What's his name?"

"Russell Brown, Corporal Russell Brown. I'll get him."

After introductions, the pair headed to the Bauer farm in Captain Meredith's jeep.

"Corporal Brown, we're on a mission for Colonel Gaskins, so all of this is hush-hush, you understand?"

"Yes sir."

"We're going to have dinner with a German farmer and his family. But first you'll see if you can fix Herr Bauer's tractor. Given the food shortage, we need to help farmers whenever we can."

"Understood sir."

"I know the family quite well as they provide me with information on the local situation. You think you can fix the tractor?"

"Sir, I've been working on tractors since I was knee-high to a sow's belly. I'll definitely find the problem. Fixing it will depend on whether I need parts and if we can get them."

"Good."

Corporal Brown and Herr Bauer were out by the barn working on the tractor while Johnny and Lorelei were meandering around the field, supposedly inspecting the crops, something they often did.

"You haven't heard who this Nazi is?" Johnny asked.

"No. I haven't heard a name. Has anyone else given you or the colonel a name?"

"No."

Lorelei gently took Johnny's hand in hers. He let her and they started walking hand in hand. No harm he thought. Lorelei had been a big help in framing the upper composition of his list of Nazi party members and SS Officers beyond those who were well-known internationally. Lorelei was smart, smarter than he was, and at five-eight, blond, and one hundred thirty pounds, she was lovely. He couldn't figure out why she was not married but thought it too impolite to ask.

"Your wife, do you love her or was it just a wartime romance?"

"Of course I love her," Johnny said. Truth be told, he didn't want to think about it. It seemed so long ago, but he held on to it—to the fact that he was married—and he behaved accordingly. Lorelei leaned over and gave him a quick kiss on the lips.

"Lorelei, any thoughts you have of us being lovers are just a will-o'-the-wisps."

They kept holding hands. *We'll see*, she thought, *we'll see.*

"I think you should concentrate on looking for this Herr Becker and ignore the other Nazis," Lorelei said.

"Why? He seems a bit far down my list."

"He's from Munich. It's a reasonable guess since he has friends here who will hide him. And it's easier for your MPs and other Amis to remember one face than to look for dozens. Can I see your list?"

Despite Lorelei's helping Johnny come up with the list, he had never shown it to her because some names on the list came from other informers. He was the one responsible for picking the Nazis to go after. He was reluctant to show the list to anyone other than Colonel Gaskins.

"I don't have a copy. Colonel Gaskins has the only copy. He's the one who decides," Johnny lied.

Johnny liked Lorelei a lot, but the colonel had explained that secrets were best kept to oneself—unless the other person absolutely needed to know. He remembered the conversation.

"Johnny, I worked with British Intelligence for a few months. Got to be pals with a bunch of the top folks. They were continuously telling each other secrets, which weren't secrets that the other person needed to know. I was flabbergasted. What one knew, they all knew. God help them if even one of them is a communist spy. And at least one of them will be, mark my words."

Lorelei and Johnny headed to the barn. As they approached the barn, Lorelei stopped holding Johnny's hand. The tractor was running.

"Captain Meredith, thank you for bringing Corporal Brown. As you can see, he's gotten the tractor running," Herr Bauer said.

"You're welcome. No problem getting it going, Corporal Brown?"

"No sir. Herr Bauer had an extra trailrod with all his tractor parts, and that's what I needed."

They went into the house for supper.

Dear Mom & Dad,

*I've told y'all about the Bauer family and my inter-
actions with them. But I haven't told y'all how I came
to know them. I was driving on the outskirts of Munich
when I saw someone pulling a coffin by a rope on the
street. I had to pull over to help this person. That's how
I met Lorelei—yes, she was pulling the coffin.*

"Miss, Miss," I said.

Lorelei stopped. It was clear she was tired.

*"What do you want?" Her tone was off-putting.
"If you want—" She started unbuttoning her blouse; I
wanted to cry.*

*"Stop! What I want is to help you with your coffin,
Miss. Nothing more."*

"I don't need your help."

"Miss . . ." I gave her a look. "What's your name?"

"Bauer, Lorelei Bauer."

*"Miss Bauer," I said as I walked up to her and but-
toned up the top two buttons she had undone, "if you
don't let me help you, I'll push you into that mud puddle and give the children who pass by one shiny penny
for every mud ball they throw at you."*

*I thought she was going to push me into the mud
puddle, then we both burst out laughing.*

We loaded the coffin onto the jeep, and I drove her

three miles farther. We talked as if we had been friends for years, and she invited me to supper with her family. She told me to stop in the middle of nowhere.

"This can't be the spot."

"A hearse will be here anon."

"I'll wait with you."

"Suit yourself."

At one point I asked, "Who's in the coffin?"

"What?"

"Who's in the coffin?"

"Ah . . . a soldier, a Waffen-SS soldier."

Her face showed distress, so I didn't ask anymore. Fortunately a swarm of beautiful butterflies engulfed us, leaving us distracted by the experience. It seemed magical and put a smile on Lorelei's face.

A good bit later, a hearse drove up and stopped sixty feet afore us. Two men got out, went to the front of the hearse, leaned against it, and waited.

"You can go, Johnny."

"They don't seem very friendly."

"I know them. Not everyone is comfortable around the Amis."

She gave me the quickest of hugs, and I was on my way.

Love,
Johnny

Johnny was at his desk reading files on various Germans. His door was open as usual. When he looked up, the woman was standing in the doorway leaning against the door frame—in profile—like a Greek siren.

"Mrs. Dietrich, this is a surprise," Johnny said as he stood and walked over.

"Johnny, I don't think formalities between us are necessary, do you?" Marlene said with a bit of twinkling mischief in her eyes.

"Now, now, behave, Marlene," Johnny replied.

"What's the fun in that?"

Johnny gave Marlene a hug.

"You were great in *A Foreign Affair*," Johnny said.

"Not yet . . . not yet . . . three more years."

"Ah . . . of course. I jumped the rope." Despite being in the Army, Johnny thought the word *gun* was in too many idioms.

"Good to see you."

"You too. You and the troupe were certainly brave to follow US troops fighting their way through France, putting on shows for us sometimes only a few miles from the front. I remember your friends joking that you were trying to get them killed."

"Fiddledeedee. They needed some real-world experiences to appreciate how good they have it."

"Are you here to put on a show for the Germans?"

"No, silly man. I left Germany what, fifteen years ago? Many Germans consider me a traitor for abandoning Germany. I'm not really very popular with certain people. If I were a Jew, they would understand my leaving. But I'm not, so they don't. I'm here to ask you a favor."

The pair were standing in the doorway, and soldiers—not believing their eyes—slowed down when walking by. Johnny didn't invite Marlene into his office, not with files about Nazis all over the place. Besides, she was enjoying the attention.

"What's the favor?"

"I understand you know Bert Bauer."

"*Know* is an inapposite word in this case."

"Ah . . . college boy. You don't have to try to impress me. You already have, remember?"

Ignoring the misplaced innuendo, Johnny continued. "I've met Bert, but only once. I know his brother and his brother's family."

"Perhaps you can get Bert to stop sending me so many letters—sometimes fifteen a day—always at least five or ten."

"Good gosh. Is that a problem? You like attention."

"It is a problem because of Harold."

"Harold?"

"Yes. Harold is my mailman, sixty-five, and his mailbag is getting too heavy. All of us on Harold's route agreed to get people to stop sending us so much mail to lighten his load. And considering the amount of mail I get, everyone is counting on me to make a big effort. Don't make me blackmail you."

At that, the two MPs walking by stopped. Marlene winked at them, and they continued on their way, smiling at each other as Johnny grimaced at Marlene.

"Johnny, don't be angry. It doesn't do to be fussy in these times. Besides, I could blackmail you. After all, you did almost shoot me."

"And whose fault would that have been? You, roaming around the woods between the American and German lines, or me, the good soldier keeping a lookout as I was supposed to."

"I told you; I got lost." As two lieutenants approached, Marlene continued, "But that was a lovely supper we had by the fire after you had me undress."

The two lieutenants looked at each other, at Johnny, then

hurried on their way.

"You're having fun with this, aren't you?"

"What do you mean?" Marlene shrugged with a coy expression. "It was nice. After all, my clothes had been ripped to shreds walking in the woods all day. The warmed-up Spam over the fire was delicious. And thanks for letting me wear your uniform that night. I had wonderful dreams. Can I tell you about them?"

"No."

"Aw . . . too bad."

"I'll see what I can do anent Bert's letters. As a matter of fact, I have an idea. Hold on a second." Johnny walked over to his desk, opened a drawer, pulled out one of the photos Marlene had given him, and walked back to Marlene. He handed her a marker. "Sign this—to Bert, Love, Marlene."

Marlene took the photo with one hand, held it on the wall, and signed it with her other hand.

"I'll use it as a lure . . . see if I can get him to cut back on the letters."

"Thank you, Johnny."

Then she hugged Johnny and kissed him on the lips right when Colonel Gaskins was walking by.

The colonel stopped and cleared his throat.

"Ah . . . Colonel Gaskins, this is Marlene Dietrich. Marlene, this is Colonel Gaskins, my boss."

"A colonel, maybe I should kiss him too."

They all laughed.

"I must say, Mrs. Dietrich," Colonel Gaskins said, "I love that photograph of you marching through the streets of Paris wearing pants when you arrived for a visit in 1933."

"Thank you, Colonel. I probably would have worn something else but for the fact that the prefect of Paris saw a picture of me wearing pants on the ship coming over to France and commented that a woman couldn't wear pants on the streets of Paris as it was illegal. So what could I do? He forced my hand."

After a few more pleasantries, Marlene said goodbye and was on her way.

"Should I ask how you know Mrs. Dietrich?" Colonel Gaskins asked.

"No sir."

"Fine. But next time I do want my kiss; at least I'm not married," Colonel Gaskin said as he walked away.

By the end of the day, rumors were flying. Johnny even got a call from a general at Army headquarters in Frankfurt asking him what was this about him and Marlene Dietrich. He told the general that Marlene had started a fund in the mid-1930s to help people leave or escape Germany. She had donated all her salary from one of her movies to get it started—which was true—and since he was in Germany she wanted his help running the fund—which wasn't true.

"You want what?" Captain Meredith said to Hans.

The two were sitting on some rubble on the outskirts of Munich at dusk.

"A cartoon of cigarettes. I have to pay bribes. A small price to pay, Captain, for a complete original file of Nazi membership cards."

"How do I know you have the cards?"

"I don't have the cards, but I will find out where they are. Once I know, I'll want twenty boxes of cigarettes."

The captain didn't flinch at twenty boxes. He had expected

Hans to ask for more. He had more than twenty boxes in storage, under guard.

"Hans, I need more proof or you're not getting a thing."

"Okay. I have seen the cards, but they are moved around periodically. I pulled one out as proof."

Hans handed the card to Captain Meredith. He took the card, pulled out his flashlight, and looked it over.

"Hmm . . . this certainly is an original. But . . . wait . . . Hans . . .this is your membership card. Hans?"

"What? You want me to give you the card of some other poor schmo? He could turn out to be some high-level Nazi . . . then what? You'd find me in a ditch somewhere. Or better yet, hanging from a lamppost at the city gate, as the Nazis were wont to do."

Johnny gave Hans the carton of cigarettes.

Dear Mom & Dad,

> *The American soldiers' frustration at how long it's taking to get back home is intense. It's a formidable task as you can imagine. There have been demonstrations by thousands of soldiers throughout Europe and the Pacific. In 1945 there were more than eight million US soldiers, and they are projecting that by mid-1947 there will be fewer than seven hundred thousand. The Army is gravely concerned they won't have enough soldiers. As a result they have come up with some goodies for soldiers who reenlist for two more years—which I did.*
>
> *I enjoy my work here and feel I'm helping a*

desperate part of the world get back on track. And as you would expect, I am keeping a journal and expect to write a book about the experience one day. Until next time.

Love,
Johnny

Dearest Clarissa,

Okay, bad news first. I have signed on for two more years over here. The good news, the Army will pay for visits by family members. And they will grant seventeen-day furloughs and pay for part of the cost of European travel. Most soldiers go to the Riviera. Let's figure out a time you can visit.

Have you noticed that our letters are getting delivered more quickly? That's thanks to the women of the 6888th Central Postal Directory Battalion. "Six Triple Eight" they are called. The battalion is composed of more than eight hundred Black women who are currently stationed near Paris. They work around the clock in three shifts to ensure we soldiers get our mail as soon as possible. When you come for a visit, let's be sure to go to Paris and thank the ladies personally— not all eight hundred, of course. I wonder, could we, all of them?

I hope things in Iowa are going well and you're not too bored watching the corn grow.

Love,
Johnny

Johnny was driving in Munich to meet a friend, perhaps his best friend, Captain Dillion Shepard. They had spent most of the war in the same company, but Dillion had been transferred to US Army Headquarters in Frankfurt several months prior. Much of the rubble had been cleared from the streets, but most buildings were still in pitiful shape. When Johnny arrived at the bar, Dillion was already at a back table. Because it was very early, no one else was there except the bartender.

"Johnny."

"Dillion, great to see you." The pair shook hands, hugged, and sat down.

"I heard you re-upped for two more years. Not surprised. The historian in you wants to be where the action is. Verily, so did I."

"You? I'm surprised, considering all your complaining—the Army this, the Army that."

"Yeah, well, when I go back to the States, I'm expected to join my father-in-law's insurance company and sell homeowner's insurance. I get bored as heck just thinking about it. Talk about dullsville. But what about you? You enjoy your work here?"

"I do. For example, it's a long shot, but I'm hoping to get all the original Nazi party membership cards for you guys in Frankfurt."

"I don't suppose Colonel Gaskins is aware of this project?"

"No, he likes initiative."

"I didn't think so."

"Why do you say that?"

"The original Nazi party membership cards are already in Frankfurt. We have them. The colonel knows that."

"What? You sure?"

"Yeah. I've been in the files. They were at Nazi Party head-quarters in Munich. At some point they were moved to a paper mill to be destroyed, but only a few of them were. The mill ran out of something or other they were using to destroy the files. The cards were smuggled out of the paper mill over a month's time. A night watchman smuggled some out each night and took them to a drop-off."

"At least it only cost me a bit more than one carton of cigarettes."

"It was quite an operation. Another German, after retriev-ing the cards from the night watchman, rendezvoused with two OSS agents who brought them to Frankfurt. Crazy thing though; the OSS agents always arrived in a hearse, and the cards were in a coffin."

Dillion kept talking but Johnny wasn't hearing.

"Johnny, Johnny . . . "

"Huh? Oh, sorry. Something else . . . I got distracted by something else. On other matters, can you find out if Frankfurt has a file on Generalmajor der Waffen-SS Schmitt? At the mo-ment he's at the top of my list of Nazis to watch for. I have his picture but very little information on him."

"Sure, I'll call you later this afternoon."

A few minutes later the friends parted.

Johnny was driving slowly and passed a man he recog-nized. He pulled over.

"Bert, Bert Bauer. Remember me? We met at your broth-er's house a few months back."

"Ah . . . let me think. Yes, Captain . . . something or other."

"Meredith, Captain Meredith."

"Yes. Sorry I didn't remember."

"Quite all right, Herr Bauer."

"Please, call me Bert. Herr Bauer is my brother."

"Fine, Bert it is. Would you like to get a beer with me?"

"Ah . . . Captain, this must be a test to see if I'm a real German. After all, what German would turn down a beer?"

"Right you are. Hops in. I know a place."

After a ten-minute drive, Johnny pulled over and found a place to park amidst the rubble. They walked into the almost-empty bar in the basement of a former hotel and ordered two beers.

"So, what are you up to, Bert?"

"Like most days, I'm heading to the black market. I have goodies to exchange for cigarettes. Then I'll exchange the cigarettes for food."

"What kind of goodies?"

Bert eyed Johnny with a bit of suspicion.

"Bert, I'm not an MP. We're friends."

Bert pulled some German military medals out of his pocket and laid them on the table.

"Ah . . . yes, we Amis like to collect these."

"Not like us Germans, who throw them into the trash as quickly as we can, as if they are contaminated. I was going to a market that the Amis frequent."

"I'm glad I ran into you."

"Oh."

"I've got something I need you to do for me. Well, it's not for me; it's for Marlene."

"Marlene . . . you know Marlene?"

"Yes, she's a friend of mine. Once she found out I know you, she gave me something to give you."

Bert's eyes were radiant. He was almost drooling.

"What, what?"

"First, you need to stop sending her so many letters. You

can only send one a month. Since she is getting so many letters from Germany—your letters, Bert—the police think she's a Nazi spy, so they watch her all the time. If she only got one letter a month, they would decide no, she's not a Nazi, and they would stop watching her."

"Of course, of course. Anything for Marlene. What do you have for me? What did she want you to give me?"

Johnny pulled out the picture and gave it to Bert. Bert's face looked like a five-year-old on Christmas morning. "I . . . I . . ." Tears were running down Bert's face.

They talked and talked, and Bert had a few more beers. Johnny was still working on his first.

"Have you heard of any high-level Nazis around, Bert?"

"No . . . no. And I haven't seen General Schmitt in ages, if that's what you're getting at."

"General Schmitt?"

"Yes, Generalmajor der Waffen-SS Schmitt, Lorelei's husband."

Johnny had to catch his breath. Lorelei's husband? No, certainly not. This trip to Munich was certainly full of surprises, more than he could process. Thoughts were bouncing around in Johnny's head, but he didn't have time to organize them. He had a meeting with Hans at their usual spot in thirty minutes. He dropped Bert at the market and was on his way.

"Captain Meredith, good afternoon."

"Hans." Johnny nodded.

"My latest update on the cards. I have discovered—"

"Hans, I'm not interested in the cards anymore. Someone else is handling that. I have another assignment for you. If you can do it, I'll give you five boxes of cigarettes. You interested?"

"Of course, Captain."

"There are rumors all over about a high-level Nazi in the area. I need information about him."

"I wish I had known you wanted this information. I know who; I just don't know where."

"Who?"

"Five boxes?"

"Yes, I'll bring them next time."

"Can I get that in writing?"

"Hans."

"Okay, okay. It is Generalmajor der Waffen-SS Schmitt."

"What? Are you sure?"

"Yes, yes. I've seen him myself. I just don't know where he is at this moment. Perhaps five more boxes if I can get that information?"

"Yes. If you can tell me where he's at and where he's going."

"Okay. I'll meet you here tomorrow, but later, early evening. And Captain, I suggest you bring ten boxes."

Johnny agreed and went back to the base. It was six when a call came through from Dillion.

"Johnny, it was great to see you today."

"You too. What's the information?"

"Yeah, we have a file on your General Schmitt. It's a very thick file."

"Can I come up tomorrow early and review it?"

"Yep, as long as your security clearance is A-7 or higher. They're in building AB-12."

"Thanks. My schedule is tight tomorrow; I won't stop by to say hi."

"Okay. I'll inform the front desk you're coming and which room the file is in."

"Thanks. Good night, Dillion."

The next day, in the late morning, Johnny walked up to the information desk on the first floor of building AB-12 in Frankfurt.

"Sergeant, I'm Captain Meredith. I'm here to review a Nazi file."

"Yes sir. We were notified that you were coming. I need confirmation of your security level."

Johnny pulled out the letter indicating his clearance level of A-7.

"Okay. Second floor, room 214. You can take those stairs. Sergeant Wilson will help you, sir."

"Thanks Sergeant."

Johnny proceeded up the stairs to room 214 and walked into the room. The waiting area was small and had a long built-in counter with several men going about their duties: making notes, filing papers, checking off items on a list. A door to the left of the counter led to the room with the files.

"Sergeant Wilson," Johnny said.

One of the men stopped what he was doing, and Johnny walked up to the counter.

"Yes sir?"

"I'm Captain Meredith. I'm here to review a file."

"A couple of rules, sir. The files cannot be removed from the room, and I must stay with you while you look at them. Just a precaution you understand."

"Of course."

They entered a large room with filing cabinets along the walls and tables in the center. Various other personnel were in the room.

"What's the last name you're looking for, sir?"

"Schmitt."

Johnny followed the sergeant to one of the cabinets.

"It should be in this cabinet."

Johnny pulled out the drawer and thumbed through the files until he came across a label—Generalmajor der Waffen-SS Schmitt. He pulled out the hanging file; only one piece of paper was in it. It was blank except for the handwritten letters "FTF." Johnny turned to Sergeant Wilson.

"Sergeant, something is wrong. This is the only paper in the file, and I was told yesterday that it was a thick file."

"Sir, FTF means 'for the fire.' We have an oil drum out back. If someone has clearance, they're allowed to take the file out back and destroy it."

"When was this?"

Sergeant Wilson looked around and called out, "Sergeant Jackson?"

The sergeant walked over.

"When was the file on Generalmajor der Waffen-SS Schmitt taken out?"

"Don't even have to look that one up. It was less than ten minutes ago."

Johnny took off running for the door.

Sergeant Jackson yelled out, "But Captain, it's . . ." By then Johnny was out the door. "Oh well. I tried."

Johnny ran down the stairs and turned into the hallway leading to the back. Johnny finally burst through the double doors and then stopped to get his bearings. He glanced around at what looked like a huge backyard, well-manicured. Near the back of the lawn was a barrel, and a man in a long coat standing in profile was throwing papers into the burning barrel.

"Stop! Stop, I say!" Johnny said as he ran toward the man.

When Johnny was within twenty-five feet of the man, the last of the papers on Generalmajor der Waffen-SS Schmitt fell into the barrel. Johnny gradually slowed down and stopped a few feet from the man.

The man turned to Johnny.

Johnny stood up straight and saluted. "Sir."

The man saluted back. "Yes, Captain Meredith, is there something I can do for you?"

"No sir. Nothing."

"That's not my impression, Captain."

"Begging your pardon, sir, I've been in the Army six years now, and, well, I just wanted to be able to tell my children that I've met General Eisenhower, sir."

"Well, let's shake then," General Eisenhower said as he removed one of his gloves. "And how many children do you have, Captain?"

"None, sir. I've been in the Army, away from my wife, for a long time. But I expect to have some someday."

"All my best, Captain Meredith. And if I can do anything for you, have Colonel Gaskins call me. He has my number."

Johnny, startled that General Eisenhower knew he worked for Colonel Gaskins, took a chance and asked, "Sir, with all due respect, why were you burning that file?"

"What file?" General Eisenhower replied.

Johnny thought for a moment while looking at Eisenhower, who evinced no emotion. Johnny said, "It's been a pleasure to meet you, sir."

General Eisenhower nodded. "You too, Johnny," he said with a wink and walked back into building AB-12.

On the drive back to Munich, Johnny had all kinds of thoughts ricocheting in his noggin: How did General Eisenhower know his first name? Why was Eisenhower—personally—destroying the file on Generalmajor der Waffen-SS Schmitt? Would Johnny be able to find out information about Schmitt from other sources? Was General Schmitt really married to Lorelei? Was the file being destroyed within minutes of his arrival in Frankfurt a coincidence?

Johnny pulled up to the regular rendezvous spot to meet Hans. A few minutes later, Johnny saw Hans climbing down from a hill of rubble.

"Captain Meredith, I have your information." Hans proceeded to unfold a map of Bavaria on the hood of the jeep as he eyed the ten boxes of cigarettes in the back seat. "Generalmajor der Waffen-SS Schmitt is at this address currently." Hans pointed to the street number and name written on a corner of the map. "But they're about to leave to meet up with a German plane right here." Hans pointed to the location on the map. "He'll board an old Junkers 52 sitting in an unused field and be flown to Italy, where he'll continue on to South America. The field is fifty kilometers from here. My understanding is the general, an SS major, and the pilot will be on their way anon. No one else is at the field, as they didn't want to risk drawing attention to the area." At that, a German sitting atop a wagon pulled by a mule stopped twenty-five feet away. "Can I have my cigarette boxes? Curt over there," Hans said, pointing to the man on the wagon, "is going to help me haul them away."

"Hans, you seem to have discovered a lot in one day."

"Captain, I told you I've seen Generalmajor der Waffen-SS Schmitt before. I went to the bar where I'd seen him a few times. Turns out the guy who was to drive him and the major to the Junkers didn't arrive, and none of the others knew how to get there. The bartender knew I grew up in that area, so I got invited into a back room to explain to the SS major how to get there. While we waited for someone to bring a map, they were reviewing the whole plan."

"Okay. Let's load up your cigarettes." Johnny felt it was worth taking the chance.

After the boxes were loaded on the wagon and Hans and Curt headed on their way, a jeep with a couple of MPs came driving by. Johnny flagged them down. They were two of the MPs he had driven to the base months earlier, so they were acquainted. He explained the situation, and they started for the Junker 52.

When they were close to the field, Johnny pulled off the road into some trees, and the MPs did the same.

"Okay, the field should be fifty yards this way. Follow me," Johnny said.

When they reached the edge of the field, they stopped. Three figures were walking across the field. The Junkers was at the far end of the field and wasn't running.

"If possible, no shooting unless they shoot. Let's start running toward them on my signal. No noise, no shouting 'Halt.' Let's see how close we can get before they spot us."

"Yes sir."

"Go."

The Amis got halfway to the Germans before they took notice. Then they took off toward the Junkers. The Germans went through the door in the back of the plane. They were hurrying to get the plane started and off the ground and hadn't closed the rear door. Moments later Johnny was through the door with the MPs following.

"Hands up," Johnny shouted as the three Germans ran up

the aisle toward the cockpit. He fired a warning shot into a seat cushion. The three stopped and lifted their arms into the air.

"First person, keep your arms up, turn around, and come back this way.

When the man, who was the pilot, reached Johnny, Johnny removed the pilot's Lueger and pushed him on to the MPs. The MPs handcuffed him.

"Okay, next. Turn around and walk this way."

Johnny recognized the man. It was Generalmajor der Waffen-SS Schmitt. Johnny took his gun, and he was handcuffed by the MPs.

"Okay. Major, same thing. Keep your hands up, turn around, and walk this way."

The major didn't move. His arms were still up. He was facing away from Johnny. Johnny repeated his command. Still no movement. Johnny walked forward until he was standing right behind the major.

The person wearing the Waffen-SS hat and uniform with the rank of major turned to face Johnny. It was a woman.

A look of complete and utter astonishment came over Johnny's face.

"What the bloody hell? You . . . it can't be."

"Hi Johnny . . . yes, it's me, but I can explain. I'm with the OSS."

"But . . . you've got a lot of explaining to do—a lot."

Johnny turned to the MPs and instructed them to take the two captured Germans to the jeep. He would be along. He lowered his gun.

"Come along," Johnny said to the woman.

A few minutes later the six of them were at the jeeps.

"You two," Johnny said to the MPs, "take those two to the

brig. I'm taking this woman to Colonel Gaskins. We've got a few things to clear up."

No one spoke while Johnny drove to Colonel Gaskin's office. Johnny didn't speak because he was still in shock; the woman didn't either—because at the moment—she didn't think anything she said would help.

Since it was a Sunday, Johnny didn't have to stop a thousand times on the way to the colonel's office and explain why the Waffen-SS officer wasn't in handcuffs. The door to the office was opened, so Johnny and the SS major walked in.

The colonel, sitting at his desk, looked up, then stood up.

"Uh . . . what's this? Why isn't she in the brig?" the colonel asked.

"You don't know her?" Johnny replied.

"No. Why would I?"

"She's OSS."

"Who told you that?"

"She did."

"And you believe her?"

"Of course I believe her. This is Clarissa Meredith, my wife."

"What! Your wife? I thought you had been writing and receiving letters from her. How did that work?"

"I have no clue, Colonel."

"Colonel," Clarissa said, "or should I say, Archangel, I was told to contact you in an emergency. I'm Spear of Destiny."

"Good heavens. The top OSS agent who infiltrated the Waffen-SS and a woman to boot. Mrs. Meredith, I must say you certainly have my admiration and your husband's too, I'm sure—once he regains his senses. Did we interrupt one of your operations?"

"Yes, Johnny did. But the duck's out of the pond now."

Duck's out of the pond?

"Those things happen, Colonel. Especially when the right hand doesn't know what the left hand is doing. Not uncommon in intelligence work. We were tracking the network that is smuggling Nazis out of Germany to Italy, then to South America."

The colonel wrote out a note and buzzed his aide, Major Burns.

Major Burns knocked on the door and walked into the office.

"Sir?"

The colonel walked over to Major Burns and handed him the note. The major read it.

"You understand?" the colonel asked the major.

"Yes sir."

"And right away, Major. Everyone might as well be at the party."

"Sir, she's already here. She's in reception, looking for Captain Meredith."

"Oh? Bring her up."

"Yes sir. The major nodded and walked out the door.

The colonel was back in his chair behind his desk.

"So, Clarissa—you don't mind me calling you Clarissa?" the colonel asked.

"Not at all."

"I'm curious. How could you carry on correspondence with Johnny over the years?"

"I didn't. My sister in Iowa was getting the letters from Johnny; she was writing him back and signing my name."

Johnny was shaking his head vigorously as if trying to remove the golly-wobbles from his mind.

There was a knock at the door. Major Burns opened the

door and stood there. The colonel nodded. Major Burns stepped back from the door, and Lorelei walked into the office.

"What's she doing here?" Johnny said as he stood up.

Lorelei walked over to Johnny and hugged him. Then she turned to Clarissa, her arm still around Johnny's waist, and said, "Finally we meet. Hello, Spear of Destiny. I'm Joan of Arc. Somehow it seems fitting that I should ask you for permission . . . permission to ask Johnny to marry me."

"What in the blazes!" Johnny said.

"Hello, Joan of Arc," Clarissa said to Lorelei. "Do you love him?"

"Yes, very much. I want to be his lover, his friend, and have his children."

"Good God," Johnny said as he slumped into his chair.

Lorelei gently touched Johnny's head and brushed his hair back several times. "Sorry for the shock, sugar," she said.

Lorelei looked at Clarissa and said, "He was faithful. I tempted him energetically —because I love him—but I failed."

"That's very noble of him. You've got quite a man."

Johnny, incredulous, got up and stumbled to the couch in the office and lay down.

"I daresay I should be jealous, but I'm not . . . inasmuch as we're not married."

"What?" both Johnny and Colonel Gaskins said simultaneously.

"Johnny and I aren't married; he just thinks we are because of an elaborate subterfuge the OSS put on several years ago."

At this point Johnny felt sure he must be dreaming.

"I can't marry Lorelei. She is married to Generalmajor der Waffen-SS Schmitt."

"Schmitt is dead," Clarissa said.

Johnny turned his head toward Clarissa. "What are you talking about? He's in the brig as we speak."

"Johnny, I can assure you no one by that name is in the brig. I've already signed an affidavit that he's dead. I was with him when he died. Let me ask you, are you in love with Lorelei?"

Johnny looked at Lorelei. "Yes, I am," he said.

There was a knock at the door; it opened, and in walked General Eisenhower.

Both Colonel Gaskins and Captain Meredith jumped to attention and saluted.

"At ease," the general said. "Have I missed all the fun?"

"Fun?" Johnny said.

"Captain Meredith, I'm confident one day you'll look back on today's events and smile. Now, are we ready for the marriage ceremony?"

"Marriage ceremony? You can marry people?" Johnny said, utterly baffled.

"Yes, temporarily. The secretary of state of Maine can grant anyone a temporary license to officiate a wedding. Here's my official letter—signed. And this base is considered US territory at present, and I have designated it as being in and following the laws of the state of Maine. So, there you go."

"Unbelievable, unbelievable," Johnny said while shaking his head.

"Lorelei, if you come over here and take Johnny's hand, we'll get started," General Eisenhower said.

"General, sir, I can't marry Lorelei; she's married to Generalmajor der Waffen-SS Schmitt. Despite the fiction that he's dead, I saw him less than an hour ago. He's in the brig as we speak."

"Captain Meredith," General Eisenhower replied, "I just

came from the brig. I can assure you there's no Generalmajor der Waffen-SS Schmitt in the brig and there never has been. The only person there is a corporal who was drunk and disorderly."

Everyone in the room was looking at Johnny.

"Oh yes, Captain Meredith, I invited a friend of yours to attend," Captain Gaskins said.

Marlene walked into the office.

"Hello, Johnny. Congratulations," Marlene said.

"Good God," Johnny said.

"Not quite," Marlene replied, "but close."

The next morning Lorelei stood over Johnny, looking down at his sweet smiling face when his eyes opened. Before he realized where he was and why, he said, "Lorelei, you won't believe the dream I had."

Lorelei smiled. "I think I would, sugar."

The End

The Un-Central Intelligence Agency

"You're asking me to volunteer to spend four months in the African jungle tracking communist rebels during the summer with no electronic equipment and no ability to contact anyone at the UIA or anyone for that matter?" Kiril asked.

"Yes," said Carver, the HR Director of the UIA. "Technically you're on loan to the government of—"

"On loan?"

"Our Republic can't be seen to be involved. Kind of like *Mission Impossible*: if you or Tracy are caught or killed, the secretary will disavow any knowledge of you and your mission."

"Tracy?"

"Tracy Path. She's an agent too. But as we're wont to say, she works on the other side of the building—separate division—which is why you don't know her. She's already volunteered. You and Tracy were picked to 'volunteer' because you both hike and camp and thence have skills such as reading maps, using a compass, living in the out-of-doors, and such.

Well, that and the fact the President of the Republic insisted the UIA's two best agents volunteer. The country you'll be working in will give you some support starting the mission but none during the mission. When you return, you'll get four months off with pay; then you'll be promoted to Commissar."

"You know I hate that title, Commissar."

"Everyone is aware of that by the way. But the position of Commissar triples your salary. You and Tracy—she's got the same deal—would be the youngest Commissars in the history of the organization. No one in their thirties has ever achieved that rank. As a matter of fact, the youngest person ever appointed to the position was fifty-five."

"How old is Tracy?"

"Two years younger than you—twenty-eight. And I've saved the best for last. There's another benefit to being a Commissar. You know how UIA missions are chosen?"

"Assumed they are from a committee of all the top people."

"No. Commissars choose. They alone decide what mission to undertake. And no one, not your boss, not the Director of the UIA, not even the president of the Republic, will ever know why you chose that mission or the mission's details unless you tell them. As you know missions are reviewed by the Committee of Affirmation when completed. Each Commissar is only required to provide enough information for the committee to decide whether the mission was successful and whether it helped the Republic. Each Commissar decides how much to tell the committee. The number of successful missions is instrumental in determining the Commissar's budget for the next year—and their pay by the way."

"Good gosh! Why would missions be chosen that way?"

"A myriad of reasons. Some make sense; some don't. But that's how it is. Gives the Commissar a lot of sway."

"I'll say."

"So, you volunteering?"

"When can I meet Tracy?"

"When you arrive in Africa."

"Since my life will hinge upon her, I want to meet her before deciding."

"No can do. But she's the best agent in the UIA."

"Better than me?"

Carver nodded, "If my life had to be in her hands or yours, I'd pick hers."

"Are you serious?"

"Uh-huh."

"Maybe I'll stop playing chess with you during lunch."

"Let's not be untoward."

One Month Later

Kiril stepped off the small plane that had just landed on a concealed airstrip in the jungle.

"Kiril, I assume. I'm General Franco: welcome."

"Afternoon, General," Kiril said as he shook the general's hand. "Is my partner here yet?"

"Tracy, yes. She's been here three days. She's been practicing. Follow me."

The pair weaved their way through an assortment of men and women in various stages of training: hand-to-hand combat, learning weapons, studying maps taped to dry-erase boards, and more. The general stopped in the middle of a group engaged in hand-to-hand combat interspersed around various obstacles, including a sizeable mud puddle.

"We'll have you and Tracy do a test run, a week in the jungle before you head out. Ah, here's Tracy," the general said, glancing over Kiril's right shoulder.

Kiril turned around to see someone almost totally covered in mud.

"You must be Kiril," Tracy said as she held out her hand.

Kiril reached over to shake Tracy's muddy hand, whereupon she grabbed his arm and flung Kiril into the mud.

"Welcome to Africa," Tracy said.

Kiril smiled. Now he was covered in mud too. He held out his hand.

Tracy reached down and pulled him up. Tracy pulled hard; their bodies smacked together, cushioned somewhat by the mud that covered their bodies—their faces now only inches apart.

"In our business you must be ready for surprises, especially here. Carver said you were second best. Don't let me down," Tracy said. She let go of Kiril and turned to the general. "We'll get cleaned up and report in, in an hour."

The general nodded.

Tracy walked toward her hut, stopped, and turned to Kiril. "Well, come on."

When they reached the hut, Tracy said, "This is our hut; follow me." She walked around to the back of the hut, stepped into an outdoor shower surrounded by a five-foot privacy partition—which of course was only partially effective—took off her clothes, draped them over the partition, and turned on the shower.

Kiril was averting his eyes as best he could, but Tracy started talking to him, so he looked—at her face.

"Kiril, we'll be together for four months and could be killed anytime. I imagine we'll often see each other naked, so averting your eyes isn't necessary and could be dangerous. This is just work. Understand?"

"Sure do, yes."

"Later today and tomorrow I'll bring you up to speed. We'll spend a week in the jungle. We'll travel to a location on the map, then return by a different route. A trial run to see what we've got the hang of and what we don't."

"Sounds fine."

"It's not fine, Kiril. The jungle's a bitch. You need to expect the worst, ready to make life-and-death decisions on the fly. Don't know if you're up to it."

"And you are?"

"I wouldn't have ended up in the mud within seconds of meeting my partner; I'll tell you that."

Kiril thought he would need all of his energy getting by in the jungle, not dealing with his partner. Now he wasn't so sure. He realized why Carver hadn't let him meet Tracy beforehand.

Tracy said, "After you shower, get dressed. Your backpack's in our hut." Tracy turned off the shower, wrapped a towel around herself, and went inside the hut. Kiril showered, then went inside. He unpacked his backpack and got dressed. Tracy was studying a map, paying him no mind.

After a few minutes Tracy said, "Tomorrow we'll spend a few hours with a British ex-army medic who's familiar with the tropics. He'll review some nonmedical points too, like how to hang our hammocks in the trees—best way to sleep in the jungle."

Three Weeks Later in the Jungle

Tracy and Kiril had already found the first of several communist rebels' weapons stashes they were searching for. They were running low on some items, including water. The two of them decided to veer off and pay a quick visit to the village of

Ioin. A disparate village, it was the one place General Franco told them they could visit without arousing any suspicion. Foreign hikers were often passing through on their way to other places. Some foreigners even lived there and set up businesses. As a result Ioin had some unusual items for a village in the jungle, including electricity. The village was five miles away.

"I'll follow the river and enter Ioin from the south. You cut across here," Tracy said, pointing to the map, "and come in from the north. We'll meet up at a place called Home Away from Home."

"Home Away from Home? What's that?" Kiril asked.

"You'll see. I was telling General Franco about one of my hobbies. He laughed and told me I should go there if I have the chance."

Kiril measured his questions to Tracy, as she often responded with the tone of a scolding teacher.

Several hours later Kiril was entering Ioin from the north. He rambled through the village and came upon a building with all kinds of arcade sounds radiating from it. A sign Home Away from Home hung above the entrance. Kiril wandered in and found Tracy playing a game on an Xbox.

"This is your hobby?" Kiril asked.

"Yes," Tracy said without taking her eyes off the screen. "Call of Duty. Go pay the man and you can play too."

"I don't play video games."

"What? Never?"

"No."

"What, Mommy and Daddy wouldn't let poor little Kiril play video games?" Tracy responded, her eyes still on the screen.

"Had other things I wanted to do."

"Like what?"

"Like learning Latin so I could read Cicero in the original. Like mathematical puzzles to expand my thinking. Like studying rhetoric so I could respond to fools. Like studying constitutional law and early American history so when I was thirty, I would understand the purpose of the second amendment of the US Constitution, something Supreme Court justices don't."

Tracy looked up at Kiril—perturbed—as she had told him one of her great uncles was a Supreme Court justice.

Bang, bang!

While Tracy's eyes were momentarily on Kiril, her character met an unfortunate end. Call of Duty was over.

"You—"

Kiril cut in. "The jungle's a bitch."

Tracy ignored the comment, grabbed her backpack, and headed out of the building. When Kiril got outside, Tracy was rocking in one of the rocking chairs on the porch.

"The store over there," Tracy said, pointing, "is where you can get water and other food items. The place next door has medical supplies. I'll meet you here," Tracy pointed to a location on the map, "in two hours." Tracy stood up and marched off.

Two hours later Kiril and Tracy met up. Tracy acted as if nothing untoward had happened, which is what Kiril expected. She always focused on what was coming, not what had been.

Four Months After the Jungle Mission

"Kiril, good to have you back," said Carver. "I hope four months off was enough."

"More than enough. Very nice."

"Good. You have a new office, badge, and title: Commissar One. Volunteering for that mission bumped you up to One. Commissar Two was bumped down and is fit to be tied, but that's that. This is a file on the agents who will work for you."

"I would have thought Tracy would be Commissar One."

"She resigned. She's already moved back to her hometown to live with her parents and sisters." Carver looked downcast as he spoke, as if he didn't want to tell him.

Kiril sighed, slightly shaking his head.

"You don't seem surprised," Carver said.

"No, not really; I hoped my feeling was wrong. Tracy and I had found the last of the communist rebels' ammunition dumps, and we were a two-week journey from our base. We knew from documents we discovered that four rebel groups were heading toward us. We had to get out quickly as we were close to being surrounded. Something—insect, animal, who knows—bit me, and I was either unconscious or delirious for three days.

"Tracy carried me, pulled me, dragged me, I don't know what all, through the jungle. I don't see how she did it, considering how far we had come when I regained consciousness. When we got to the base camp, Tracy was in the camp hospital—if you can call it that—for five days. I stayed with her. She would often turn melancholy, talking about her parents, sisters, growing up, all out of the blue, seemingly without realizing it, then abruptly stop. The doctor assured me she was fine; she just needed rest.

"On the plane back to the Republic, we agreed to meet at a café, and we did on the Friday after our return. She spent most of the time talking about her parents and sisters again. When we said bye she seemed distant, sad. I haven't seen or spoken to her since."

"Sorry, Kiril."

"Do our reports on the mission match?"

"In general, yes."

"In general. What does that mean? Are they different?"

"No, not really. Tracy included things in her report you didn't."

"I can understand during the days I was unwell. But what else?"

"Kiril, you know I can't disclose what is in someone else's mission report."

"Well . . . how many things were different?"

"Two. She included two things you didn't," Carver said, despite knowing that would tell Kiril what he wanted to know.

Kiril knew right away what the two things were; he was shocked. They had agreed not to report anything about the missionaries. And as far as Tarzan and Jane were concerned, Kiril thought it was understood; they would not report that.

"Wanting to be with her family and sisters was why she left the UIA. You just need to get on with business."

Shortly after Kiril left Carver's office, the Director of the UIA walked in. "Things all set with Kiril?" the Director asked.

"Yes sir."

"He ask about Tracy?"

"Yes. Not surprised that she's gone. He hoped she was still here, working on our side of the building as a Commissar."

"Did you tell him Tracy completely blew the African mission to save his life?"

"No, why be cruel."

"Courageous woman. She could have walked away, left Kiril in the jungle, and saved herself and the mission. I was stunned to learn she told one of the rebel groups she encountered that she was from Russia and was sent to Africa to evaluate their efficiency. Good thing she speaks Russian, then giving them the map of the ammunition stashes she and Kiril had located to show them that their security was lax. And naturally they moved the ammunition. Probably wasn't easy convincing the rebels to carry Kiril most of the way back to the base either. That had to be tough for her, destroying over three months of hard work in arduous conditions."

The Director and Carver talked more about Tracy and her assignment.

Two Months Later

Kiril drove to the first gate that surrounded the UIA building. Nothing else was near; the building sat in the middle of a field. The first obstacle he confronted was a chain-link fence with rolled barbed wire on both sides. Kiril showed his ID, then put his hand on a fingerprint reader. The gate for the car opened.

Two minutes later he arrived at the second perimeter—a wall. He looked into a viewer for a retina scan. The steel doors opened.

One minute later, the road went underground into a short tunnel with a titanium door at the exit. He stopped and turned off his car, removed his left shoe and left sock, opened the car door, and put his foot on a foot scanner—toe prints.

"Ick . . . gee whiz, Jackson. What's with the goo on the foot scanner?"

"Sorry, Kiril. Commissar Two must have spilled his syrup smoothie. He just came through. Didn't say a word."

"Why am I not surprised."

"Hold on; I'll get you cleaned up."

Jackson ran into the office and got a bucket filled with

warm water, foaming soap, several towels, and a footstool. He ran out, planted the footstool, sat, and cleaned off Kiril's foot. Jackson liked Kiril. Everyone did, so Kiril was treated right. Well, that and the fact Kiril was the only Commissar whose agents were licensed to kill—just like James Bond. *Why tempt fate?* Jackson thought.

"There you go, Kiril." Jackson opened the titanium door. Once the door opened, Kiril drove out of the tunnel into the compound, parked, and entered the building. The guard handed him what looked like a Popsicle with a long wire.

Kiril took it and dropped it on the floor, apparently accidentally.

"Ah . . . would you look at that. Bob, get a new one out of the sanitizer, please."

"Sure thing, Kiril."

A minute later, Kiril had a new Popsicle in his hand and placed his tongue on it—tongue prints. The door opened.

Two Years After the Jungle Mission

Dear Carver,

I hope you and your family are well and that things are great at the UIA. I understand you're no longer getting reports on me. I'm fine and my sisters are doing great. They're wonderful, especially the toddler, Siobhan, as you can imagine.

You're underrated. We both know Kiril wasn't the second-best agent in the UIA and that you paired me with him despite the request of the President of the Republic. But you knew what you were doing—something I didn't realize at first. I thought he was like most other men, but no, he's in a class by himself. He saved my life more than once, and I his. Did you know he believes one of the ten commandments should be Thou shall not treat woman any less than a man, in all things, and in all ways. God, I can't believe how badly I treated him, at least at first. I appreciate your kindness through all of this. I hope he's well and happy. If you have the time, I wouldn't mind knowing how he's doing.

Your Friend,
Tracy

Since Carver wasn't getting reports on Tracy anymore, he was grateful for the letter. Albeit he did grapple with twinges of regret about Tracy moving away and Kiril not being allowed to be privy to all that transpired.

Dear Tracy,

Thank you for your kind words. You are the best— just rough around the edges, which it sounds may have been smoothed. I believe Kiril was good for you, but I regret that the mission was so arduous. Kiril was third best at the time, so I don't feel I was negligent in regard to the mission's requirement. I don't think Kiril not knowing all that happened was the best course of action, but my hands are tied, so to speak. I have no doubt he'd want to know. Maybe one day we can tell him. Kiril is doing fine, an outstanding job so far as Commissar One. I'm sure you picked up on the fact he likes to know things. And of course, he's studying or doing something productive when he's not at work.

He's written a book of short stories under the nom de plume Anson Meredith. He's not married or seeing anyone, and he likes children. I know he and your youngest sister, Siobhan, would get along fabulously. All the best. And write anytime.

Your Friend,
Carver

Four Years After the Jungle Mission

"So," said Wyatt, Kiril's second in command, "we going after this guy Noel Lizfin?"

"Yes," Kiril responded. "He owes the Republic money. This should mostly involve the computer guys finding him. Don't imagine it will take long. Should be a quick mission unless the guy has died. Here's the file they need to track him down."

"Okay. I'll get the geeks started," Wyatt said, and he left Kiril's office.

Several hours later, Wyatt knocked on Kiril's door.

"Come. Ah, Wyatt, got anything?"

"Some. But we're at a dead end unless you want to sign a Class A authorization waiver."

"I need to do that?"

"Noel Lizfin is in the witness protection program. Seems he testified against some corrupt politicians a while back."

"I see. You have the authorization form for me to sign?"

"Here you go. Figured you'd want to do it."

Kiril signed the form.

"I'll get them started," said Wyatt.

Several hours later Wyatt knocked on Kiril's door.

"Come."

"Here you go: his new name, address, etcetera. He lives here in town, believe it or not."

"Well, lucky for us. Does the Marshals Service still have him under surveillance?"

"Can't tell. You want the guys to keep digging?"

"No. I'll go see Noel and collect the money. It shouldn't be a problem."

"You? But if we do get into trouble with the Marshals Service, Noel Lizfin will be able to identify you."

"He has a moderate case of prosopagnosia. A lot of people do."

"A case of what?"

"Didn't you read the file?"

"Not that close."

"Noel has face blindness. Unless I hung around him for a week or two, he wouldn't recognize me, even if he saw me the next day."

"I assume you'll want him to pay in cash. Will he have that much on him?"

"A guy in witness protection. They always have cash—and lots of it. They might have to do a runner and live on the lam for months."

"Want me to check out a gun for you?"

"No, you know I hate the things. I can't imagine I'll need it. Might as well go now. First, I'll type up an invoice, and I'll be on my way."

An hour later Kiril pulled up to the curb a few houses down from where Noel Lizfin lived. He strolled to his house and knocked on the door.

"Yes, can I help you?" Noel asked after he opened the door.

"Yes, you can, Mr. Lizfin. I know that's not your name now but—"

"Look, Buddy! if you don't leave—"

"Steady on, steady on, Mr. Lizfin. No need for concern," Kiril responded as he showed Noel his UIA ID.

"The Marshals Service know you're here?"

"Don't know, don't care. A small matter to see you about; then I'll leave. No harm. Can I come in?"

Noel sighed, "Follow me."

They walked back to the kitchen and sat at the breakfast room table.

"Mr. Lizfin, I'm here to collect money you owe the Republic—after a fashion."

Kiril laid the invoice in front of Noel, who took a minute to review it.

"You want me to pay this?"

"Yes."

"Now?"

"Yes."

"I don't suppose you'll take a check?"

"Considering how long you've gone without paying it, No."

"Okay, I'll get the money. Be right back."

"Oh, and Mr. Lizfin, don't try and contact the Marshals Service. My agency has all your communications shut down until I leave."

"Ah . . . it's less trouble to just pay you. You can understand that."

"Forsooth."

About three minutes later Noel came back into the kitchen.

"Here you go," Noel said. He counted out the money while Kiril watched.

Kiril opened his briefcase and deposited the money.

"I don't suppose I'll get a receipt?" Noel asked.

"No."

"I should thank you; I'm gonna sleep good tonight."

"Conscience bothering you?"

"Conscience, no. It's just . . . well . . . what chance do murderers, robbers, and blackmailers have if the most secret intelligence agency in the world is going after a guy for a twenty-five-year-old overdue library book fine of $541.17."

"Point taken. I'll see myself out. Cheers."

The Following Afternoon

"Congratulations, Kiril. I understand the Committee of Affirmation gave you another point for a successful mission. Collecting money from a guy who disappeared years ago and owed the Republic money. How much did you collect?" Carver asked.

"You know I can't tell you that."

"I understand you decided not to tell the Committee of Affirmation the amount either."

"You know Commissars have leeway in the number of details we provide to the committee," Kiril said.

Six Years after the Jungle Mission—Kiril's Office

"I picked up an interesting tidbit at lunch today," Wyatt said.

"Oh."

"Turns out Huck, the newest member of our team, is Commissar Two's nephew."

"Who told you that?"

"Alice."

"She's one of the more dependable gossipers," Kiril replied.

"Maybe Commissar Two is stepping up his game, leaving

aside those childish pranks he pulls on you occasionally, trying to get you fired instead. After all he hates you for taking his Commissar One position; plus, for years now you've had the highest number of successful missions of any Commissars. Maybe you should have Carver transfer Huck to another Commissar or have him fired."

Kiril looked at Wyatt with an expression that conveyed *And what would I say about that?*

"Okay, you'd say, 'Don't judge someone until you have all the facts.'"

"Having him fired; that would be inhumane. As far as the transfer, we'll see. For the time being, let's get him out of the building for a while. Being new, he should go on a mission so we can evaluate his surveillance skills."

Kiril walked over to one of the bookshelves and pulled down a telephone directory.

"Gracious! They still publish those?" Wyatt asked.

"A regular phone directory? Some places do, but you have to ask for them."

Kiril sat at his desk, closed his eyes, opened the phone book, randomly placed his finger on the page, then opened his eyes.

"Tilly Flowers, 146 Willow Grove Lane. We're going to put her under surveillance, 24/7 as a training mission to evaluate Huck. Huck takes the day shift and no coming to the UIA during the operation. And get Charles to handle the night shift. Have them send in reports daily."

"Okay, I'll get it set up to start tomorrow."

"Fine."

Four Weeks Later

Kiril and Wyatt had wrapped up their morning meeting. "What do you want to do about the Tilly Flowers surveillance?" Wyatt asked.

"Oh yeah, it's been what—four weeks. That should be a good enough sample to judge Huck's ability for surveillance. Have you reviewed the material?"

"No," Wyatt responded.

"Do that today. Let me know how Huck did."

"Okay."

Midafternoon Wyatt knocked on Kiril's door.

"Come. So what do you think?" Kiril asked.

"I'm reluctant to say."

"That bad?"

"It's more of an issue of believability."

"How's that?"

"Tilly Flowers is a communist spy."

"Gee whillikers."

"And, get this; she happens to be Commissar Two's mistress."

Kiril ran his hand through his hair. "My, my, what a happenstance."

"Now what are you going to do?" Wyatt asked. "We can't keep a lid on this."

"I need to review the surveillance material before we do anything."

"I thought so. It's in file 2317C," Wyatt said.

"Pull up a chair," Kiril said to Wyatt. "I'll put it on screen."

Later that day Kiril was in Carver's office telling him about Tilly Flowers.

"You can see by the surveillance why we reached the

conclusions we did about both Tilly Flowers and Commissar Two," Kiril said.

"How is it you put Tilly Flowers under surveillance?"

"Random training mission to evaluate Huck. Picked her name out of the phone book."

Incredulous, Carver just stared at Kiril for fifteen seconds.

"If it was anybody but you, I wouldn't believe that. Did you know that Huck is Commissar Two's nephew?"

"Yes, and wondered why you didn't tell me."

"Didn't think I needed to, you being the egalitarian you are."

"In that case, there was no harm in telling me."

"I reckon you're right."

"What happens now?"

"The inquiry will need to be handed to someone on the other side of the building. Commissar Two will be placed on administrative leave until the inquiry is completed."

"And Huck?"

"That's up to you, Kiril."

"Has the makings of a good agent. See no reason he shouldn't remain on my team."

"Good."

Two Weeks Later

Kiril was walking down the hall in the UIA Headquarters and turned the corner. There, ten feet in front of him, was Commissar Two.

"Ah, Commissar Two, you back?"

"Yes," Commissar Two said as Kiril reached up and shook his hand.

"Glad to hear it. Imagine you're eager to get back to work."

"I am. And thank you."

"For what?"

"For the 'keep your chin up' card you sent me and the family. You're the only one who bothered while I was under a cloud."

"Until all the facts are known, we need to support each other. We're on the same team after all."

"You're right. And thanks again, Kiril," Commissar Two said. That was the first time he ever called Kiril by his name. "Oh, by the way, how is Huck doing?"

"I think he's going to make a fine agent, Evan," Kiril said.

Evan nodded and continued to his office.

Later that day Kiril and Carver sat at a table playing chess and eating lunch in Carver's office.

"I see Evan's back, Kiril said as he moved a pawn.

"Evan, I do declare. No more Commissar Two?"

"Not since he started calling me Kiril."

"I guess a leopard can change its spots."

"You going to tell me what happened with him and Tilly?"

"You know I can't."

"So, you going to tell me what happened with him and Tilly?" Krill knew that Carver would give if he kept asking.

"Tilly Flowers is a double agent."

"Wow. Didn't see that coming. I thought we weren't allowed to do any of that double-agent stuff."

"The other side of the building can. And they keep it close to the vest, which is why I didn't know."

"And Evan?"

"Evan knew she was a double agent as he is her contact outside the office. That's because they have been good friends since high school, so their meetings wouldn't raise any red flags."

"Hope my surveillance didn't blow her cover."

"Actually it gave her more credibility. The UIA wouldn't be spying on its own agent."

Fourteen Years Later, after the Jungle Mission

Carver was in Kiril's office with a big grin on his face, almost giddy even. "Here are three resumés for you to review. With so many successful missions, you're allowed another agent."

Kiril took the folder. "Who's the most promising?" Kiril asked as he opened the folder.

"Last one in the file. You'll want to hire her."

As Kiril flipped through the resumés, he asked, "You think she'll be good?"

"No question; she is."

"What makes you so sure?"

"It's Tracy."

Astonished, Kiril looked up at Carver. Kiril hadn't said her name in over fourteen years. Neither man said a thing as Kiril reviewed her resumé. According to the resumé–Kiril didn't know it was a feigned resumé, but Carver did—she had worked for the Drug Enforcement Administration for the prior twelve years.

"I'm confused," Kiril said. "She'd get a Commissar's position. She wouldn't be working for me with that rank."

"She's not going to be a Commissar."

Kiril's eyes narrowed a bit. "That's callous. She earned it."

"It is what it is," Carver said as he shrugged his shoulders. "Her father passed away five years ago, her mother a few months ago. Shame too, as they both were on the younger side. Tracy is the guardian of her two sisters. One's about to start college; the other's fourteen. They moved here last week."

"Wow, out of the blue. Who would have thought."

"She starts Monday."

"You hired her already—before you discussed it with me?"

"Tell me I'm wrong."

Later That Day in the Director's Office

"Your discussion with Kiril on hiring Tracy, did that go okay?" the director asked.

"No problem."

"Kiril say anything when you told him Tracy refused the Commissar's position we offered her, saying she only wanted to be an agent on his team?"

"It slipped my mind," Carver said while raising his eyebrows.

"He'll find out, don't you think?"

"Probably, but no point muddying the waters now."

"Does Tracy know the power a Commissar has?"

"She does."

"And still, she turned it down . . . interesting."

Later That Evening at Barnes and Noble

Kiril was placing a book back on the shelf, *The Price of Time* by Chancellor Edward. A book he would buy on his way out forasmuch as it snagged his interest and had a 4.25 rating on Goodreads. Then he heard a honeyed voice.

"Hello, Kiril."

He felt a jolt—as if his finger had slipped into a light socket—he turned around.

"Tracy. I wasn't expecting to see you until Monday; what a treat."

"I didn't know how you'd feel about me coming back."

"Ardor is what I'd feel."

Tracy froze momentarily, then shook it off, figuratively speaking.

"Oh, these are my sisters. This is Nadine."

"Hello," Kiril said as he shook her hand.

"And this is Siobhan."

"Hello to you too, young lady."

"Hello, Mr. . . ."

"Kiril, please. I feel we already know each other; besides, Siobhan is my favorite name."

A big grin manifested on Siobhan's face. She glanced at Tracy and stepped forward to hug Kiril.

"Siobhan and I will be looking around," Nadine said. "We'll meet you two in the café, anon." The two walked off.

Kiril and Tracy walked to the café.

"*Anon,* I like that word," Kiril said.

"I know. Sometimes I think the hardest thing for you in the jungle was four months sans a dictionary. Well, after dealing with me, that is."

"*Sans*—you remembered that word."

"Always, and your eyes as you said, 'Sans you, I'll never—'"

"Can I take your order?" the man behind the café counter said.

Kiril and Tracy smiled at each other and ordered their drinks. After they got their drinks, they went to a table and sat down.

"The family would like to invite you to the house this coming Saturday afternoon," Tracy said.

"Wonderful. What time?"

"About two."

Tracy and Kiril continued catching up until Nadine and Siobhan joined them at the table.

The Following Saturday

Kiril arrived at Tracy's house and pulled into the driveway. He was about to ring the doorbell when Siobhan opened the door.

"Welcome, Kiril," Siobhan said as she hugged him.

He hugged her back.

"Tracy's in the shower, and Nadine is cleaning up the kitchen. Let's go to the living room, shall we?"

The living room felt more like a cozy den than a room used for entertaining.

Siobhan started at one end with the shelves full of pictures in frames.

"This is one of my favorites," she said. It was a picture with a pregnant mother, a father, and two daughters, Tracy and Nadine, standing behind them. It was probably taken several months after Tracy left the UIA.

As they continued around the room, Kiril said, "What in the world is this?" pointing to what looked like a Roman bust.

"That's something Tracy bought at a Goodwill store."

Kiril went over and lifted the bust. "Gosh, it's heavy. Maybe it's the real thing."

"From a Goodwill store. I wouldn't think so," Siobhan responded.

"Siobhan," Nadine called. "Can you help me a second?"

"Be back in a minute, Kiril."

After Siobhan left the room, Kiril snapped several pictures of the bust from different angles with his phone. Then he wandered into the hall. As he walked, Tracy came out of the bathroom wrapped in a towel and almost bumped into him.

"Sorry, just wandering around," Kiril said.

"Oh . . . well then, follow me."

As Kiril was following Tracy, he said, "Where are we going?"

"To my bedroom. I've got something to show you."

When they entered the bedroom, Tracy turned to Kiril and said, "Voila!"

"Wow!" Kiril said.

"Do you like?"

"Absolutely. I've never seen so many Van Goghs in one place. There must be at least twelve or more. And some of my favorites."

"One of the things we have in common—a love of Van Goghs. And your favorite and mine, *The Starry Night,* hanging over the bed."

"Oh," Siobhan said as she entered the room. "This is where you got off to. Sorry to interrupt your assignation, but let's let Tracy get decent."

"She looks decent to me," Kiril said.

Tracy smiled.

"Come on," Siobhan said as she pulled Kiril out of Tracy's bedroom.

It was ten o'clock when Kiril left for home. He couldn't remember when he'd had such a nice time.

Six Months After Tracy Returned to the UIA

Kiril knocked on the door of room number 714 at the Hotel Absinthe. The hotel overlooked the embassy of a communist country; well, communist in a negligible way. Kinda like every other country in the world that says it's communist but isn't, using the term for a worker's paradise to enslave its people.

The door opened a few inches until the small chain was taut just below eye level. Tracy peered out. She closed the door, removed the chain, and let Kiril in.

"Sir," Tracy said as Kiril entered the room.

"Isn't this Wyatt's stakeout?"

"We swapped."

Kiril let out an inaudible sigh. He wasn't going to ask Tracy if she was up to speed on the case or if she knew what they were looking for. By far she was the most sagacious and dauntless agent in the UIA. It would have been an unnecessary slight to ask. She always knew the details and was never nonplussed.

"You think we'll find out anything today doing this?" Tracy asked.

"Never know. Might as well have a go. You know as well as I do that sometimes the information is handed to you—if you're paying attention."

"Aunt Tasty is catering the noon lunch later today—a big affair. I'm kinda surprised that she was chosen to cater it when her restaurants only serve soup."

"Lucky for us, I'd say, since that one soup of hers is world-renowned. We'll take any opportunity that comes our way. We got a microphone into one of her aprons, but will she wear it today? With all the brouhaha, perchance our target will get careless and let information slip. I see you're using the newest telescoping microphone. Didn't know we were using them in the field yet."

"We're not. Coaxed the lab into letting me give it a try."

"Good for you. If Aunt Tasty doesn't wear the apron, we'll have to rely on this new equipment."

"Yes we will."

"I'd hang around a bit, but I've got a meeting with Carver," Kiril said.

"See you later then," Tracy said as she let Kiril out.

Later that day there was a knock on Kiril's office door.

"Come," Kiril said as Wyatt entered the office. "Any luck at the stakeout?"

"Almost, but no cigar. Tracy dropped off a recording. Listen to this conversation between the ambassador, Aunt Tasty, and others—we're unsure who."

" . . . yes, well, no harm in telling you. The secret is . . . " After that, shrill electronic sounds were heard.

"Aw . . . someone turned on the electronic jamming at an inopportune moment. Take the recording to the lab. See if they can clean it up." Kiril said.

As Wyatt grabbed the recording, there was a knock at the door.

"Come," Kiril said.

Pavel, a member of Kiril's team, entered.

"Kiril, Wyatt," Pavel said. "I have something from the phone tap. The ambassador and Aunt Tasty have planned a picnic together tomorrow at noon in Seminole Park."

"Hmm. She made quick work of cozying up to the ambassador," Kiril said.

"And get this," Pavel said, "the ambassador insists no bodyguards."

"I bet they'll be bodyguards there whether or not the ambassador knows. No head of security will take a chance on him getting mugged or worse. Have the team start watching the park at seven in the morning so we can identify his security detail beforehand. Then a full-court press on the surveillance teams with microphones: a couple on a blanket, the kite with the microphone dangling from it, and someone taking their pet for a walk. Plenty of work for everyone. What's the name of the new guy we've got?" Kiril asked.

"Wally."

"Okay. Let Wally handle walking the pet."

"You want Tracy in on it?" Pavel asked.

"No. The three teams—that should be enough. We'd be wasting her time. Who do we have lined up as the guest helper for the taping of Aunt Tasty's cooking show tomorrow night?

"Fred," Pavel responded.

"Okay."

"Tomorrow, in the park," Wyatt said, "you think the secret will come up again since it's already been mentioned?"

"Could be, maybe for clarification or more details. Maybe Aunt Tasty is going sweet on the ambassador."

"I'll leave you two to it," Pavel said as he left.

"Wyatt, let's you and me meet at the park tomorrow and watch the operation. Dress very casual, shorts and T-shirt."

"Okay. See you then," Wyatt said as he left.

The Next Day

Kiril and Wyatt sat on a bench and looked over Seminole Park. It was around eleven thirty. The agents on the blanket were in the center of the park, a straight shot in all directions for their listening device. Sam had his kite flying and was wandering around, waiting for the ambassador and Aunt Tasty to arrive before he settled on a spot to plant himself.

"Where's the new guy, Wally?" Kiril asked.

"He should be here anon. Said he had to take his pet to the vet first."

"Wish I hadn't been on vacation when he was hired. I haven't even met him yet. Have you met him?"

"Yeah."

"How does he seem?"

"You're asking me; you know better. Anyone who wants to be a spy is a bit off, including you and me."

Kiril shrugged.

"There's Wally now," Wyatt said.

"Where?"

"Over there, on the edge of the park." Wyatt pointed.

They both watched Wally for a few minutes.

"Where's his dog?" Kiril asked.

"Don't see anything yet. Maybe he's let it run loose. But look, over there." Wyatt pointed. "The ambassador and Aunt Tasty."

Sam started moving slowly, trying to line up the kite directly over the couple. The UIA couple turned toward the pair to line up their microphone. The early UIA team had located the two bodyguards for the ambassador and informed the team.

"Over there's Wally," Kiril said. "I still don't see a dog near him."

"He didn't tell me it was a dog."

"You couldn't do this with a cat. What kind of equipment did he requisition this morning?"

"A small transmitter and some superglue."

"Superglue? Maybe gluing a transmitter to the dog's collar?"

Four school buses pulled up to the curb. Students carrying band instruments started getting off the buses.

"Uh-oh," Kiril said. "I don't like the look of that."

"I'll go over and find out what's going on."

"See if you can spot Wally's dog while you're over there."

"Will do."

A few minutes later, Wyatt returned. "What's the story?" Kiril asked.

"The band has permission to practice in the park for two hours, marching, playing their instruments."

"That's great . . . just great. And Wally?"

"He's got his pet with him."

"If it's a dog, it must be as small as a chipmunk."

"It's a turtle."

"A turtle! Good gosh. You sure?"

"Oh yeah."

"Look, Kiril. Wally's picking up the turtle and walking toward the ambassador and Aunt Tasty."

As Wally got close to the target, but not too close, he started to put the turtle down but dropped it. Both Kiril and Wyatt involuntary flinched. Then Wally picked up the turtle, brushed it off, and put it back down.

Kiril, shaking his head, said, "Wyatt, I'm going home to change, then go back to the office. You keep an eye on things. Come by my office later, and we'll review what we get. I'm not optimistic."

"Okay," Wyatt said as he got up to wander around the park.

Kiril got up and headed back to his car.

Later Kiril was back in his office waiting for Wyatt to review whatever had turned up at the stakeout.

Wyatt knocked on the door.

"Come," Kiril said. By Wyatt's expression, Kiril could tell the day's mission was unsuccessful. "Like I thought?"

"Yep. The lab's reviewing the data, but I doubt we have anything. The band's marching and playing interfered with the microphones, and the sight line of the couple was never adequate. A hawk mistook the microphone dangling from the kite for lunch and absconded with it. And Wally with the turtle . . . I'll let him explain."

At that Wyatt called Wally and asked him to come to Kiril's office and give his report.

"Wally, you get any useful transmissions today?" Kiril asked.

"No sir. I dropped Valdosta—"

"Valdosta?"

"Yes sir. My turtle, Valdosta."

Kiril looked at Wyatt, expressionless. "Go on."

"I didn't realize it, but the transmitter that I superglued onto Valdosta's shell broke his fall, but it also broke the transmitter. Didn't know that until the operation was over."

"Okay. That's all," Kiril said while he thought back to Wyatt's comment in the park about spies being a bit off.

"Thank you, sir. And sir, if you ever need to know anything about turtles, I'm your man. Sea turtles, land turtles, big—"

"Yes, Wally. Thank you. You can go now."

Wally left Kiril's office.

"I pulled Fred off the assignment for Aunt Tasty's cooking show tonight. I gave it to Tracy," Kiril said.

"Why?" Wyatt asked.

"This is dragging on too long. I want to wrap it up. I'm confident we can get the information off Aunt Tasty's phone, and who better at that than Tracy."

"Makes sense. Does Tracy know?"

"Yeah. I called her a bit ago. She's going to drop by on her way to the event."

"Okay. I'll check with you tomorrow."

"Yep. See you then."

A little later there was a knock on the door.

"Come," Kiril said.

"I've got an hour before I need to go to Aunt Tasty's. Any last-minute updates?" Tracy asked.

"You're wearing that?" Kiril said, not quite believing what he was seeing and what he was *not* seeing.

"You referring to this diaphanous blouse? What's wrong with it?"

"Let me rephrase my question. You forgetting something?"

"A bra? Don't need it; they're not that big. But seriously, I'm gonna need an enticing distraction, and all Aunt Tasty's assistants are men. I need them looking at something other than my hands. That gadget I have to attach to her phone will take a whole minute to download her data. Speaking of busts, I assume today's stakeout was one?"

"Very funny, but yes, it was. I would wish you luck, but you of all people don't need it."

"Aw . . . you say the sweetest things."

"And speaking of busts, I've been meaning to talk to you about yours."

Upon hearing that, Tracy walked around to Kiril's side of the desk, pulled herself up on it, her braless bust near Kiril's face. She crossed her legs and casually started swinging her leg with the red high heel. "About time."

Kiril pulled out his phone, tapped it several times, and turned it to Tracy so she could see the photo.

"Oh, my Roman bust. How exciting," Tracy said in a disillusioned tone of voice.

"It's real. Either the son of Pompey the Great or Nero Claudius, a Roman commander. They're not sure which. And they want it back."

"They?"

"The German state of Bavaria. A Bavarian King owned it. About eighty years ago, it was in a replica of a Roman villa in the German town of Aschaffenburg. The Republic bombed it during WWII, and after the war a Republic Army base was established in Aschaffenburg. I assume a soldier either found it or bought it, brought it back to the Republic and forgot about it. He dies and it ends up at Goodwill. We'll probably never know how it came to be there. The

Bavarian Government wants it back. They're willing to give you a finder's fee."

"Good gosh! How much?"

"Don't know. Here's their number. I didn't tell them who I was or who had the bust."

The Next Day

Tracy knocked on Kiril's office door.

"Come."

"Good morning sir."

"Morning, Tracy."

"Here you go. A printout of the information on Aunt Tasty's phone. And if you note pages eighteen and nineteen—the highlighted items."

Kiril turned to the pages. "This is it; what we're looking for. Is it all here?"

"Yep. The information is all there and exactly right. The lab already did a mockup, tested it, and it passed. Here's a sample for you to check personally."

Tracy took a seat while Kiril spent ten minutes on the sample.

"Yes siree! That's it, no doubt. Great work as usual. Thanks. You have any problems last night?"

"None. All her assistants are in their twenties, raging hormones. Could have dropped a brick on her foot, cut off all her hair, pushed her into a mud puddle, and no one would have been the wiser."

"Okay. Are we ready to disseminate the information to the public?"

"Just waiting for you to give the word."

"I'll tell Carver to set up a meeting with the Committee of

Affirmation for later today. After my presentation and their approval following the completion of the mission, I'll give them the go ahead to disseminate the information."

Later That Day

Kiril was standing at the head of the conference room table about to give his presentation to the twelve members of the Committee of Affirmation.

"Ladies and gentlemen, I see that you all have had a chance to sample the prototype."

Kiril explained the mission and what they had done. Much of it was recondite, but the committee understood that.

"Let me conclude as follows. My team has discovered the secret recipe for Aunt Tasty's world-renowned soup—Tasty's Delight. And after tasting the soup yourselves, you see we did discover the recipe. There is no disputing that a person should receive some financial benefit for something they create. But Aunt Tasty's copyright on the soup—yes, she has a copyright on it—is good for her lifetime plus seventy years. And as of now, due to the success of her soup, her net worth is north of one hundred billion dollars."

There were gasps in the room.

"And that doesn't include her five hundred-million-dollar yacht, which she has only utilized for two weeks over the past twenty years."

More gasps filled the room, along with the shuffling of papers and note taking.

"Aunt Tasty has been selling that soup at inflated prices, and since the recipe is unknown, no one can make it on their own. She has been cheating the citizens of this Republic for fifty years now.

"Our founders didn't get everything right, but the copyright law, they did. They believed a person was entitled to some financial reward for their creation, as we do, but it was not limitless. In the year 1790, the first copyright law allowed for a copyright of fourteen years. The founders believed that information and knowledge should eventually be shared and benefit all citizens, not just the few.

"Some of you may be surprised by such a 'socialist' attitude by our founders—but there you go. And if you will recall, one of the coins minted at the time had the phrase *United States of America* on one side and *Liberty, Parent of Science and Industry* on the other. Many members of our legislature voted to extend the copyright to lifetime plus seventy-five years after substantial contributions from Aunt Tasty for their reelection campaign. As such, we have arranged to leak the recipe to the public."

One Year After Tracy's Return to the UIA

Kiril moved his queen, now a potential threat to Carver's king.

"I've been meaning to ask you to talk with one of our recruits," Carver said as he surveyed the chessboard.

"Why?"

"He has a bit of a different background."

"Okay."

"He'll be expecting you this afternoon at four in the cafeteria."

"What's his name?"

"Daniel."

Later That Day

At four o'clock Kiril went into the cafeteria and picked up a bottle of water. He surveyed the deserted cafeteria, which had only one occupant, and walked over.

"Mind if I join you?" Kiril asked.

"Please. You must be Kiril. I'm Daniel. Nice to meet you, sir."

As they shook hands, Kiril said, "The 'sir' is not necessary."

Daniel nodded.

"Why do you want to be a spy, if I may ask?"

"Didn't want to be a preacher like my father and grandfather. Thought it would attenuate my family's disappointment if I was doing something patriotic."

"And that's a good reason to be a spy? To placate your father, grandfather, and other family members?"

"I've always been very patriotic, and I enjoy traveling. Figure a spy travels a lot. Was traveling all the time growing up."

"How's that?"

"My parents were missionaries and traveled the world. I'm used to being in dangerous situations and don't scare easily. Think that's a good trait for a spy. About sixteen years ago my family and several other missionary families were captured by a small tribe in Africa. Our group entered the country without permission as my father was very interested in bringing Christ to the tribe. He didn't realize they were cannibals. We were caught and tied up with vines."

"How old were you?"

"Eight."

"No one had issues with taking an eight-year-old into the African jungle?"

"Not with the Lord as our shield."

"I see."

"Two of the members of the group were killed and . . . well, died. Then in a matter of hours, it seemed, the cannibals disappeared. The next morning Jimmy realized his vines had been cut. He untied the rest of us, and we got out of there."

"What happened to the cannibals?"

"Don't know. Jack Prescott, one of the missionaries, said it was clear the Lord sent them straight to hell, but I'm not so sure."

"Oh . . . you doubt the Lord sent them straight to hell?"

"Yes. I saw a woman—just for a few moments. She was Caucasian, dressed kind of like a soldier."

Looking past Daniel, Kiril noticed Tracy heading over with a drink in her hand. Kiril rubbed his lower chin with the back of his hand, then extended his index finger to the tip of his nose as if he had an itch.

Tracy veered off, and out of the cafeteria.

Daniel continued, "I always thought perhaps she was part of some army unit on a training mission in the jungle, and they got rid of the cannibals."

"Interesting. Lucky for you—whatever happened."

"Now it feels like a dream, and I puzzle over whether I would recognize the woman."

"Would you . . . recognize the woman?"

"No idea. If you don't mind, Kiril, I need to head out. I have a dentist appointment."

"Sure. I imagine we'll talk again."

Kiril returned to his office, unlocked the door, and walked in. Tracy was sitting with her feet up on Kiril's desk.

"Make yourself at home," Kiril said as he walked to the desk and sat opposite Tracy.

"Thanks, I always do. If you didn't want me, why give me a key?" Tracy winked. "Anyway, what's with the wave off?"

"Was talking to a recruit, Daniel. Carver wants my opinion of him."

"And what, he's good-looking, and you don't want any competition?"

Kiril gave Tracy a frolicsome smile.

"Sixteen years ago his family was in the African jungle with a missionary group some cannibals captured."

"Good Lord, what are the odds?" Tracy said, slightly shaking her head.

"He saw you. You must have put something in your action report about the missionaries. That must be why Carver wanted me to talk with Daniel; see if he knows anything about us being there. With the background checks they do now, Carver would know he was there when we were."

"I did put in my report. Just one sentence: 'We ran across some missionaries held by cannibals and eliminated them.'"

Kiril just looked down, then at Tracy. He wanted to say, *But we agreed not to mention the missionaries.*

"I'm so sorry, Kiril."

"Not exactly the best description of the encounter. Most of the missionaries believe God saved them."

"Well, you could say that was true . . . in a roundabout way."

"Can't figure why I didn't get any blowback at the time if that was in your report. At a minimum they would have disciplined me, or at least inquired about the incident."

"What should we do?"

"I'll talk to Carver."

"We both should speak to him, together."

Kiril stared at Tracy as he thought.

"Okay. Tomorrow we'll see if he has some free time. Let's pick up Siobhan, get some burgers, and go to Hypatia Park."

Forty five minutes later, all three were eating hamburgers at a picnic table in Hypatia Park.

"Why are we here? This isn't Hypatia Park," Tracy said.

"How do you know?" Kiril asked.

"The sign at the entrance said Hudson Park."

"This is it, Hypatia Park. Unofficially, of course. I rename places sometimes."

"Why?"

"I'm a fan of Hypatia."

"Oh. And who was she?" Tracy asked.

"Can I answer that, Kiril?" Siobhan asked.

"Certainly."

"Hypatia was a famous prominent philosopher, astronomer, and mathematician in Alexandria, Egypt, around 400 AD. She was not Christian but was tolerant of both Christians and pagans and taught both in her classes. She was on good terms with both the Bishop of Alexandria and the Roman Perfect of Alexandria, who had recently become Christian.

"The bishop died, and the new bishop spread false rumors about Hypatia. A Christian mob, possibly under orders of the bishop, killed her. The killing rocked the country for two reasons: philosophers were considered untouchable by public violence in the Roman world, and she was a woman. The City Council of Alexandria complained to the Roman Emperor, who investigated and curtailed some of the powers of the bishop."

"Well, that's quite a story," Tracy said. "We still have two hours before dusk; you want to stroll around the park?"

"Sure."

Siobhan trailed along, walking a few steps behind them.

As they walked holding hands, Tracy said, "We could go off into the woods. Pretend we're in the jungle. Play Tarzan and Jane like we did that one time in Africa."

"That's all it took, isn't it?" Kiril said.

"To fall in love?"

"To conceive a child."

Tracy stopped. "What?"

"Siobhan's our daughter; she's not your sister."

Siobhan ran up to Kiril, hugged him from behind, and said, "Finally."

Tracy, looking at Kiril, asked, "How did you know?"

"I've known since Barnes & Noble. I could just tell; don't ask me how. And when you and Nadine went to the restroom, leaving me with Siobhan, I looked at her and raised my eyebrows. She did a slow nod and winked at me. I winked back. Besides, a woman acts differently with a daughter than a sister. You did a good job hiding it from everyone with your mother's and father's help. Your mother was wearing a pillow under her dress in those photos in your den. And you were always standing behind somebody."

"I knew you'd figure it out; Siobhan's love for you is so palpable. She was ten when I told her you're her father. She's very mature for her age. I told her about us in the jungle playing Tarzan and Jane and how she was conceived. At that age she thought it was both romantic and icky. As she got older, she reminded me more and more of you. I couldn't stand it anymore; being away from you. I told the UIA I was coming back, no ifs, ands, or buts."

Tracy gave Kiril a soft, thorough kiss. The first since Africa, despite their flirting over the past year.

"Well, I guess we have more things to discuss with Carver tomorrow," Kiril said.

"More than you imagine," Tracy said as Kiril gave her a quizzical look.

The three continued their stroll around the park with Siobhan between her parents, holding their hands, with a big grin on her face.

That night both Tracy and Kiril had the same dream about what really happened with the missionaries. Perhaps it was because they both were sleeping under the print of *The Starry Night.*

"You expecting your dodgy pirate friend to be coming down the river for a stopover here?" Tracy asked Kiril.

"Yep. Six weeks ago, when Captain Bly let us stay on his boat for the night, he told me his schedule."

"You two sure hit it off. He's French, isn't he?"

"He is. And he comes from a long line, a very long line, of boat captains from Avignon, France. Knowing that, I'm sure I can get him to help us."

Tracy slightly shook her head—wondering. "You'd better be right. I hate to think we wasted our time carrying all these cannibals down here to the river after shooting them with tranquilizer darts."

"There's one more. I'll get him and be back anon," Kiril said.

As Kiril was nigh at the river with the cannibal on his back, he saw Tracy talking to Captain Bly.

"Ah, Ms. Tracy," Captain Bly said, "it's so good to see you again."

He lifted her hand and kissed it.

"Kiril and I need you to eliminate these cannibals for us," Tracy said, pointing to the natives laid out in a line on the dock.

Kiril laid the last cannibal on the dock and walked over to the pair.

"Good to see you again, Kiril. Didn't know if I would," Captain Bly said as he shook Kiril's hand and hugged him. "Tracy tells me you want me to eliminate these natives for you."

"Eliminate in the sense of banish . . . for a week, maybe two. Not in the sense of kill; definitely not kill. And I have ten thousand dollars' worth of American Express Travelers Checks to sign over for your help."

"You know I'd like to help. But I have a schedule to keep, and, well, if my customers come to think I'm not reliable . . . I could lose a lot of business."

"I understand, I do. But surely a descendant of the boat captain who sailed William of Ockham down the Rhone and out of Avignon, France, in 1328, saving him from a possible death sentence at the hands of Pope John XXII could do this favor for a friend."

Captain Bly's face lit up.

"You know: you know about what my Grand Papa did, saving Ockham and a couple of his Franciscan buddies?"

Captain Bly grabbed Kiril's face, a hand over each ear, and kissed him on each cheek as the French are sometimes wont to do.

"Of course, of course I can do this for you."

Captain Bly yelled at his men to start loading the cannibals on the boat as he went aboard to supervise.

Tracy looked at Kiril. "How did you know his grandfather, what, sixty generations back, did that?"

"He may not have. But anyone whose ancestor was a boat captain back then probably believes his ancestor was that boat captain."

"This is the Ockham of Ockham's Razor fame?

"That's him—if there are two explanations for something—pick the simpler one."

"I guess if the Franciscan Order calls the Pope a heretic, things aren't likely to turn out well. Thankfully the King of Bavaria offered Ockham protection from the Pope."

Seventeen Years Ago in Carver's Office at the UIA—Flashback

Four weeks after Captain Bly had taken the cannibals, but before Kiril and Tracy had returned from Africa, Carver had the news on. It may as well have been off; he wasn't paying attention.

"A tribe of African cannibals has been identified here," the reporter said. "Without a doubt, this is quite a shock. Not so much for them being cannibals, as they had been identified as such years ago. Rather, how did a whole tribe of African cannibals end up in the Australian outback."

The Next Day at UIA Headquarters

Kiril was walking to his office after his eight o'clock meeting with Wyatt. He unlocked his door and walked in.

"Oh," Kiril said as he glanced around his office at Tracy, Carver, and the Director of the UIA. "Hope I didn't keep y'all waiting." He had no idea they would be there.

The Director got up from Kiril's chair. "Here, take your seat," he said as he got up, pulled up another chair on the other side of Kiril's desk, and sat down next to Tracy and Carver.

Kiril sat down and saw a report on his desk titled "Nativity" with the security code *Red One* on it.

"When we're done here, we'll leave this report for you to read. Tracy can explain it in more detail," the Director said.

"This report is above her security clearance," Kiril said.

"You know," said the Director, "when the three of us arrived at your office," Tracy unlocked the door; your door. Normally that would be a significant breach of security—a subordinate having a key to their boss's office. In this case—it's not—as Tracy always has had a higher security clearance than you. Truth be told, Tracy never left the employment of the UIA after the African mission."

Kiril looked at the three faces across from him: he was puzzled.

"After Carver and I get some clarification on the missionary incident, we'll leave. *Nativity* is the reason Tracy's security clearance is higher than yours," the Director said.

Once Tracy and Kiril explained the missionary incident to the satisfaction of Carver and the Director, they left Kiril's office.

"They didn't say anything about Siobhan being our daughter," Kiril said.

"No, they didn't."

"But they know."

"Yes, they do. You going to read the report?"

"I'd rather you tell me about *Nativity*."

"Before the African mission, the other side of the building had a project called *Nativity*. The man and woman with the best genes, I was the woman and a man named Roger was the man—were to have intercourse, and I would raise the child in a learning-oriented environment—similar to what was done with John Stuart Mill. Mill became very depressed at about twenty and saw no value in his knowledge until he started reading poetry—in which he found great joy, so Siobhan's education would be broader than Mill's and include fun topics.

"I was due to have intercourse with Roger. Roger, however, refused. He refused even to provide a sample. Roger said,

'I won't conceive a child with that bi . . . ' Well, you know what I was like in those days. Then the African mission came up.

"They had started testing the genes of men on this side of the building. But we were in Africa when they discovered your genes were even better than Roger's. I had no idea until we returned. When Carver told me, I told him I was pregnant with our child—*Nativity* was back on—my assignment was back on—rules I had to abide by were back on—I'd never been so happy and sad at the same time. And now—finally—our time has come, Dear Kiril, with each other and with our wonderous daughter. I knew it would."

The End

4

The *Mona Lisa*

Artemis—Oh, excuse me.

Profusion—Quite all right. You missed my toes. No harm done.

Artemis—Airports, always busy.

Profusion—Yes, especially this one in Las Vegas.

They beheld one another.

Artemis—I know this is a bit of a cliché, but you seem familiar . . . somehow.

Profusion—Verily, I was thinking the same. There is something. Have time for a coffee? Perhaps we can figure this out.

Artemis—Sure, why not. My flight to San Francisco was delayed due to fog. It doesn't depart for three hours.

Profusion—Same for me, except it's four hours.

There was a coffee shop between gates 17 and 19.
After a few minutes they were seated in the coffee shop with their drinks.

Profusion—Maybe we met at the airport in Boston. I go through it often.

Artemis—No. I travel frequently, but never there. What about O'Hare in the winter?

Profusion—Been there, but never in the winter.

Artemis—Where are you from?

Profusion—Born in Providence, but I live in Boston. You?

Artemis—Born in Lakeland, but I live in Atlanta.

Profusion—I don't recall knowing anyone from Lakeland, Florida.

Artemis—Georgia.

Profusion—What?

Artemis—Lakeland, Georgia. Two hundred and thirty-four miles from Lakeland, Florida.

Profusion—Certainly never met anyone from Lakeland, Georgia . . . that I know of.

Artemis—Okay, let's take the easy road. What's your name?

Profusion—Profusion Presley. And you?

Artemis—Artemis Rains. I would certainly remember someone named Profusion, and I don't. Lovely name by the way.

Profusion—Thank you. And I have to say the same. I would remember meeting an Artemis.

Artemis—This is a puzzle.

Profusion—Isn't it.

Artemis—I think we're going to have to use a systematic approach.

Profusion—Sounds reasonable. It's quite a mystery to sort out.

Artemis—We've tried names. So, we should proceed through careers, then where we've lived.

Profusion—If we met in passing, the possibilities would be endless.

Artemis—But if it was just in passing, why would we have this profound sense of knowing each other?

Profusion—Must be something to it.

Artemis—What field are you in?

Profusion—I'm a lawyer and work for the International Criminal Court.

Artemis—You work at the Hague, in Holland?

Profusion—No, Boston. I have to go to the Hague on occasion, but I spend most of my time in the US interviewing witnesses. And you?

Artemis—Forensic accountant. The company I work for—No Hiding—tracks down money trails, seeing which rabbit holes it went down.

Profusion—How often are you successful?

Artemis—Every time. There's always a trail, always. It's just a matter of finding it, and we always do. My work is very satisfying.

Profusion—I bet. Does it involve crypto?

Artemis—No. And don't get me started. If there's a bigger tool for criminals, I've never seen it.

Profusion—Can't disagree.

Artemis—I don't see how our work paths could have crossed.

Profusion—Agreed. Where have you lived?

Artemis—Quite a few places, at least growing up. My father was in the Air Force.

Profusion—Aha, our first connection.

Artemis—Oh, your father was in the Air Force?

Profusion—No, the Navy.

Artemis—Hmm, not likely to have put us in the same place. Where did you live growing up, in order?

Profusion—Norfolk, Virginia; Rota, Spain; Jacksonville, Florida; Souda Bay, Greece; finally, Rockville, Maryland, when my dad was at the Pentagon. And you?

Artemis—Greenville, Mississippi; Valdosta, Georgia; Madrid, Spain; Hampton, Virginia; Wiesbaden, Germany; and finally, Fairfax, Virginia, when my dad was at the Pentagon. One place in common, the Pentagon, and two places in close proximity, Virginia and Spain.

After comparing the dates, they discovered they lived in Virginia at different times, so they ruled it out. But their dates overlapped in Spain and at the Pentagon.

Profusion—Where did you live when your dad was stationed at the Pentagon?

Artemis—Fairfax, Virginia. And you?

Profusion—Rockville, Maryland.

Artemis—Did you ever visit the Pentagon?

Profusion—Twice. Short visits both times and don't remember anything really.

Artemis—I visited once. Like yours, a short visit. Then I was in the basement five days a week for a couple of months. I worked as a Congressional intern and had to change buses there.

Profusion—Don't see how we would have run into each other there.

Artemis—Me neither. And we were both in our late teens, so it seems more likely we would remember.

Profusion—What about Spain? We both lived there from 1964 to 1969.

Artemis—Yeah, but Torrejón Air Base and Rota Naval Base are about four hundred miles apart.

Profusion—That was the first overseas assignment for my family, so we traveled a lot in Europe.

Artemis—Yeah, same for my family. I can remember some of the places we went, but not all of them.

Profusion—What about Seville; did you ever visit it? It's near Rota.

Artemis—I believe we did, but I recall nothing about the visit.

Profusion—Maybe we both were just having a moment. Or maybe we did meet and will never remember.

Artemis—But you seem so familiar. Especially your smile. You have a pretty smile, subtle.

Profusion—Thank you.

Artemis—Like the *Mona Lisa.*

Both their mouths went agape.

Artemis—The *Mona Lisa*!

Profusion—The Louvre!

Artemis—Paris, May 9, 1969. Oh my God, that was you?

Profusion—One of the most memorable days of my life.

Artemis—Mine too. But over time my image of you faded to the point that it disappeared.

Profusion—Same for me.

They stood up and hugged each other as long-lost friends.

Profusion—It's amazing that both sets of parents went to watch those museum movies and told us to peruse the museum all day.

Artemis—Sure was. Parents wouldn't do that today.

Profusion—What all did we do that day?

Artemis—A better question might be, "What didn't we do?"

Profusion—Let's see; hide-and-go-seek, tag, explorer, role-playing, pigeon chasing, and of course, my favorite—fountain splashing.

Artemis—Ah, the fountain, my favorite too. I still can't believe we snuck into the part of the museum being renovated, and no one was there.

Profusion—That huge empty room with the fountain in the middle with a replica of Michelangelo's *David* in the center of it.

Artemis—And the fountain's jets shooting streams of water toward the statue.

Profusion—Don't forget the sprinkler system in that section; it must have run for hours.

Artemis—How long did we play in that fountain?

Profusion—Hours. I'd never felt so carefree.

Artemis—I could tell. I was startled when you took your top off; even more so when your knickers came off. But I felt warm and happy inside.

Profusion—It felt like we were in a world of our own—only us in the whole wide world.

Artemis—I still remember pulling my briefs off—both of us stark naked and playing; it seemed the most natural thing in the world.

They chuckled and smiled as they recalled splashing, dunking each other in the fountain, and other foolishness.

Profusion—Do you remember the promise we made sitting next to each other in the fountain, our arms draped over each other's neck?

Artemis—Promise?

Profusion—Yes, that in ten years, on May 9, 1979, we would return to the Louvre.

Artemis—Oh my gosh! I had forgotten about that.

Profusion—I know.

Artemis—You know? Oh no, don't tell me you were there on May 9, 1979?

Profusion—I was, mostly because of the proposal.

Artemis—Proposal?

Profusion—Yes, you had promised to marry me.

Artemis—Profusion, surely not; I don't remember that.

Profusion—Just like a man, not remembering promises made to a young lady.

Artemis—If I had been there, do you think we would have gotten married?

Profusion—Who knows?

Artemis—Then the day we spent together came to a crashing end.

Profusion—Yeah. Thanks to that kooky kid Harold; what a slob. Why they let him into the museum while eating an ice cream cone with it dripping all over his T-shirt and down his arm is puzzling.

Artemis—How could I forget that.

Profusion—And he kept following us, talking nonstop. Then we split up to try to lose him.

Artemis—And we did—for a while.

Profusion—He followed me, so I walked into the ladies room. He followed me in, and a woman grabbed him by the ear and gave him a tongue lashing. I used the opportunity to escape.

Artemis—Then we rendezvoused at home base, the *Mona Lisa* and came up with a scheme in case he found us. And he did, anon.

Profusion—And you tripped him just like we planned.

Artemis—Of course we figured he'd fall down, start crying, and go looking for his mom and dad.

Profusion—Yep. But he crashed into that display case, which tipped over, shattering into a million pieces.

Artemis—It was good that the Fabergé egg wasn't in it yet. And Harold, not a scratch on him, amazing. I don't think anyone actually saw me trip Harold, but we were so close to the chaos that the guards wondered if we had something to do with it.

Profusion—Yeah. After we were taken to the administrator's office and split up, we never saw each other again.

Artemis—Funny, we never told each other our real names.

Profusion—We were just having so much fun playing make-believe.

Neither Profusion nor Artemis had realized—at least consciously—that at some point in their conversation they began holding hands across the table.

A Priest from the local parish and his associate, a Brother, were walking by the table and stopped. The Priest looked at the couple.

Priest—Well, as I live and breathe. If it isn't Profusion and Artemis.

Both Profusion and Artemis looked up. Neither recognized the Priest.

Priest—Harold, the Louve, May 9, 1969.

Profusion and Artemis were flabbergasted.

Harold—I always thought you two were in cahoots.

Artemis—How did you know our names?

Harold—I was in the administrator's office when he was talking to your parents.

Artemis—Profusion, should we?

Profusion—Should we what?

Artemis—I know I'm forty years late, but should I keep my promise?

Profusion—You don't mean?

Artemis—Yes, I do. Let's get married. Harold is a priest; he can marry us.

Profusion—You know what? Why not? I'm a believer in first impressions, and a person can't hide who he really is when you play naked with him for hours. You can do that, can't you, Harold? Marry us?

Harold—Hey, this is Las Vegas. Brother John always has some blank marriage certificates in his satchel. Nothing to it.

Five minutes later

Harold—You may kiss the bride.

A minute later Father Harold cleared his throat. It was a long and thorough kiss. After all, they had waited forty years. Artemis and Profusion stopped kissing, thanked Harold, and went to change their plane tickets. They were going to Boston. They were walking through the airport when Artemis stopped.

Profusion—What is it, Artemis?

Artemis—I did ask you to marry me in 1969, didn't I?

Profusion—Of course you did, dear.

Artemis didn't notice Profusion had one hand behind her back with two fingers crossed.

Artemis—Oh, we didn't get Harold's address. We should write him and thank him.

Profusion—We can always call the archdiocese and get it.
Artemis—Copy that; no concerns.

The couple continued on their way.
Back in the café, Father Harold and Brother John sat at the
table drinking coffee.

Brother John—I don't think you should have done that.
Harold—Why not?
Brother John—Well, when they find out you're not Father Harold, but con artist extraordinaire Harold Smith, they might come after you. And think of all the legal trouble they could get into not really being married. And it's a personal affront to me when people live in sin.

Harold—We're in Las Vegas and you're worried about people living in sin? Anyway, we'll be long gone. Did you know that in some states if two people are married by someone they think has the power to marry them, the state will, in fact, consider them married? It's not hard to imagine the church feeling that way, and God even.

Brother John—I didn't know that.

Harold—That's why I'm the boss. I know the little things. We need to be leaving and head to Heaven's Rest Nursing Home. Janet told me yesterday she would change her will this morning to include me and said she'd have a copy of the will for me by two this afternoon. The doctors expect her to go within the week.

Brother John—That's what I like about you; you go after those widows with a frenzy.

The End

5

Chicago to St. Louis by Train

The weather was slightly chilly and sunny, and the year was 1882. The train was about to leave the Great Central Station in Chicago for St. Louis. A woman on the verge of thirty-nine and a young man of fifteen were sitting in a compartment.

"Aunt Lucille, we're going to St. Louis for a bit of entertainment, but why no suitcases?" Troy asked.

"Entertainment, yes," Aunt Lucille replied. "We're going to the St. Louis Symphony tonight. They're playing Raff's Symphony No. 4 and 5. It's rare for a symphony to play those, but they are absolutely delightful. We'll catch the midnight train back to Chicago. By the way, have you read the book I gave you?"

"*Madame Bovary*, yes. I understand why you didn't want Mother and Father to know I was reading it. But why did you *want* me to read it?"

"Education, young man. Education."

"But . . . I'm not sure how—"

Aunt Lucille turned her bright blue eyes on Troy.

"Troy, never assume you know someone; how they feel, what they want, how happy they are—especially a woman. Slight grammar detour: it's fine to use 'they' when referencing one person. Back to my point, everything you think is from your point of view, and you may be mistaken. Women are often too timid to express intimacies. It's not completely their fault. It's what they grew up witnessing and what is expected of them, and the attitude is continually reinforced. As Voltaire said, 'Uncertainty is an uncomfortable position, but certainty is an absurd one.' Do you understand?"

"I think so."

"Good. Keep the book as a reminder. But don't put it on the bookshelf until you're twenty-one: otherwise, my sister will have a fit."

"You're certainly more liberal than Mother and my other aunts. How come?"

"When I was six, I had to attend some big to-do with my father. It was a large party among the well-to-do. Well-dressed people wandered around talking. Father told me to mingle about but not get in anyone's way. The party was composed of men, with the exception of one elegantly dressed woman.

"The unexpected sight of a woman conversing with men beckoned me. I drew closer to hear their conversation. I didn't understand all that I heard, but I was enthralled that the woman was holding her own. The two men finally withdrew, and I approached her."

"Excuse me," I said.

"Certainly, young lady. What can I do for you?"

"Who is this Cicero you were discussing?"

"Do you have access to a library?"

"Oh yes. My father has a grand library in his office at home."

"Well, every day you must visit the library and pull out a book to read. Don't get frustrated if it's hard. It will get easier over time."

"Then this woman gave me a short history of Cicero. Enthralled, I failed to notice that a crowd had gathered. Father was amongst the watchers.

"A few days later I asked my mother why this woman knew so much. She told me not to fret over the matter as the woman was an anomaly.

"One day some years later, Father came into his office and saw me reading a book. Usually I would abscond to my room with the book, but not that day. He went to his desk and started working. After a few minutes he came over and asked what I was reading.

"The Philosophy of Aristotle, *Father.*"

"*Oh,*" *he said with a chuckle.*

"*Yes. I consider myself a Peripatetic: notwithstanding Aristotle's views on the intellect of women, which I am confident he would unsay were he here today.*

"He looked as if deep in thought, then a winsome smile appeared and a slight nodding therewith."

"*Lucille?*"

"*Yes Father.*"

"*How many of my books have you read?*"

"*Two hundred and eight.*"

"*Two hundred and eight! Good God child. And just how do you know it's that many?*"

"*I keep a list.*"

"*May I see your list?*"

"*Yes. I have it right here.*"

"My father read through the list."

"The Physiology of Women—*you've read that book?*"

"*Yes Father. I know all about the uterus, the vagina, the—*"

"*Yes, well . . . very good, but I wouldn't mention any of this to your mother.*"

"I'm well aware of that, Father."

"Young lady, on Tuesday and Thursday evenings, and occasionally on the weekend, you and I will have a study session and talk about the books you've read. How does that sound?"

"Oh wonderful, Father! Just wonderful!"

"And perhaps I can bend the rules of the Diogenes club and have you accompany me to our philosophy discussions."

"Mother was none too pleased with this turn of events. She told Father that nothing good would come from educating a woman beyond the needs of a wife. Thankfully Father ignored her comment, so I have always loved learning and thinking for myself, which is what Father wanted. Father died a few years later, so my sisters did not receive the same encouragement to learn as I had, given I was the oldest."

A well-dressed man walked into the compartment and sat across from Aunt Lucille. He reached into his shirt pocket and pulled out a cigar.

Aunt Lucille said, "I beg your pardon, sir; please do not smoke."

"Madam, would you deprive a man of his one true vice?"

"My lungs can do sans the cigar smoke as it causes mischief in my chest. Would you smoke if Olivia petitioned you so?"

The man regarded Aunt Lucille closely, then smiled and nodded, putting the cigar back in his pocket as he realized she was quite the well-read woman since she knew who Olivia was.

Then the man noticed the book Troy was reading.

"Young man," he said to Troy, "are you enjoying the book?"

"The Adventures of Huckleberry Finn? Oh yes. Of course, it's no *Madame Bovary."*

The man burst out with a hearty laugh. "No, it certainly

isn't. Tell me, was it your illustrious sister," the man glanced at Aunt Lucille, "that gave you *Madame Bovary* to read?"

"Sister? She's—"

Aunt Lucille gently poked Troy in the side.

"Ah . . . yes sir; it was. How did you know?"

"Your sister strikes me," the man said as he glanced at Aunt Lucille, "as both a learned and beautiful woman. A woman who likes to pass on knowledge. Would I be correct?"

"Most certainly, sir."

"I would introduce myself," the man said while gazing at Aunt Lucille, "but then, you certainly know who I am as you know who Olivia is. But you are?"

"Lucille Grant, Miss Lucille Grant. And this is Troy Grant."

Troy reached up to shake hands with the gentleman.

"Ah . . . any relation to the former president?"

"Yes, very distantly," replied Aunt Lucille.

"It's my understanding that one of General Lee's nephews is on the train. But no worries; he fought for the Union."

At that, one of the train stewards slid open the door to the compartment and stepped in.

"I'm sorry for the delay," the steward said to the man. "Your compartment is ready now."

The man stood and handed Troy his card.

"If you and your sister are ever in Connecticut, please stop by. I'm sure Olivia would love to meet you both. Pleasant travels to you."

The man and the steward left the compartment.

Troy turned to Aunt Lucille and asked, "Who is Olivia?"

"The gentleman's wife."

Troy looked at the card in his hand, and his eyes widened. "Aunt Lucille, did you know that was—"

"Mark Twain, yes," Aunt Lucille said as she reached over

and plucked the card from Troy. "I think we are going to have to visit him, young Troy."

"Why?"

"Why? I'd think that would be obvious; I'd like to know what my life would be like had I met Mr. Twain before Olivia met him."

Aunt Lucille pulled out a book and started reading.

An hour or so later, the porter came into the compartment.

"Miss Grant," the porter said, "a telegram addressed to you was in the mail pouch we snagged at the last town."

Lucille took the telegram and read it.

"Anything wrong, Aunt Lucille?" Troy asked.

"Not at all. An acquaintance of mine is on the train. I'm going to see her for a while. You stay here."

A few minutes later Lucille was knocking on the compartment door of Mr. Twain.

"Enter," was the reply.

Aunt Lucille opened the door to reveal Mr. Twain reclining on the seat.

"Ah, Miss Grant," he said as he stood, "it's a pleasure to see you again and so soon. I'm surprised as I gave the porter a boodle to keep my compartment number to himself."

"I figured as much. So I asked the porter not the compartment number of Mark Twain but of the wittiest man on the train. The number escaped his lips before he realized what he had done."

Mr. Twain let out a chuckle, "You've exceeded my expectations of the capacity of the human species; that's quite a feat, believe you me."

Lucille did a slight curtsy and said, "Thank you." Then from disguised pockets in her dress, she withdrew a Colt revolver and handed it to Mr. Twain.

"Well, I must say I am used to gifts, but never have I received a revolver from a female admirer."

"It's not a gift, Mr. Twain. I want it back. I ask that you take it, hidden away of course, and go sit with Troy for a spell."

"Oh," Mr. Twain said with a puzzled expression.

"I have knowledge that two bandits are on the train, intending to rob the passengers." Lucille pulled out a badge that read Pinkerton National Detective Agency. "I'd like you to look after Troy until I've subdued the bandits."

"With all due respect, I can help subdue the culprits."

"Bellona and Heloise will help me."

"Bellona and Heloise?"

From her concealed pockets, Aunt Lucille pulled out two more Colt revolvers—one in each hand.

"I see. I know who Heloise was, but Bellona?"

"The Roman goddess of war. Besides, having you help could beget me a lifetime of trouble."

"I not quite sure how."

"Imagine the headline, Mr. Twain—PINKERTON AGENT GETS MARK TWAIN KILLED."

"Ah, yes, that would be most distressing on several accounts. I will go sit with young Mr. Troy."

Leaving Mr. Twain's compartment, Lucille worked her way up through the train until she was just outside the car with rows of passengers in their seats. She saw the two robbers with their backs toward her, pistols out, watching the nervous passengers pass around the bag to be filled with the loot. The men were standing about twelve feet from the door to the car. As she entered the train car, the robbers turned toward her. Face hidden by her hat and hair, Lucille pretended to faint and sank to the floor before they could get a look at her. The robbers shrugged and turned back to the passengers. Lucille brushed her hair aside and pulled out Heloise and Bellona. She sat up and pulled the hammer back on each colt. At the click of the hammer, both men started to turn toward her.

"Don't move," Lucille commanded. "There is a colt aimed at each of your hearts."

The robbers froze.

"Lucille, that you?" one of the robbers said without turning around.

"Corbin," Lucille said. "My, my, I don't believe we ever finished our game. Knight to g7."

"Bishop takes Knight."

"Queen to f8. Checkmate," said Lucille.

Corbin bent down, placed his colt on the floor, and pushed it to Lucille.

"What . . . what the hell are you doing?" the other robber asked Corbin.

"Davis, let me introduce you to Lucille Grant, a Pinkerton agent."

"Aye, so?"

"You remember the Bannerman gang?" Corbin said. "This woman killed the whole gang in that shootout. Her against the lot of them. We'd have a better chance fighting God."

"Corbin," Davis said, "you know I don't hold to no sacrilege against the almighty."

Davis bent down, placed his gun on the floor, and kicked it to Lucille too.

Lucille approached the two men and gave the handcuffs to Corbin, who promptly put them on Davis. Then she handed Corbin his gun.

"I guess I interrupted your operation," Lucille said to Corbin.

"Allan Pinkerton's on the train," Corbin warned her. "He won't be happy about your interference."

"Just what the hell is going on, Corbin?" Davis asked.

"Oh, shut up," Corbin replied.

"Which compartment is Allan in?" Lucille asked.

"D-3."

Lucille headed to compartment D-3 and knocked on the door.

"Come in."

"Hello, Allan."

"It's Mr. Pinkerton to you, Lucille.

"And it's Miss Grant to you, Allan."

"I suppose this means Davis is in custody and you've blown my operation? Someone at headquarters—who still favors you—must have telegraphed you about the impending robbery, not knowing it was a setup."

"Golly-gee whillikers, Allan. You're just smart as a whip. And you're welcome by the way. At least the passengers weren't robbed, thanks to me."

"You know you're not a Pinkerton Agent anymore, Lucille; haven't been for what? Fifteen years."

"It must have slipped my mind. You know how scatter-brained we women are."

"I fired you and for a good reason."

"Yes, your wife was jealous that I was spending more time with you than she was. I suppose I can't blame her. She's a bit insecure."

"Now, now, let's leave your sister out of this," Allan said. "Wait, wasn't Troy spending the day with you?"

"Yes, he is with me, but he was never in any danger. The St. Louis Symphony is playing a couple of Raff's symphonies tonight."

"Raff. Good. At least you're showing the young man some culture."

As Lucille left the compartment, she saw Mr. Twain leaning against the wall in the corridor.

"Eavesdropping is a nasty habit, yet the deed has been done," Mr. Twain said.

Lucille raised her eyebrows and smiled as Allan walked out to the passageway.

"Mr. Twain, how about you and I play some poker?" Allan asked.

"Mr. Pinkerton, I'm a bit tired. How about you save yourself the time and trouble and just pay me to keep my mouth shut."

Mr. Twain pulled out the Colt and gave it back to Lucille, then turned and walked back to his compartment.

Allan had a questioning look on his face.

"It's my gun."

When Lucille got back to her compartment and sat next to Troy, she said, "By the way, your father is on the train."

"Wow! Good thing I'd finished *Madame Bovary*."

"Indeed. I suggest you read tomorrow's paper; see what you missed."

The End

6

The Police Chief

The four members of the town council of Bane, Maine, were on the phone with the Los Angeles chief of police.

"So, Chief, you'd recommend we hire Mr. Blane as our chief of police?" asked Mike Smith, the head of the town council.

"He should be fine handing out parking tickets, rescuing kittens in trees day in, day out."

The council members looked at one another. Mike loudly cleared his throat. Silence ensued.

"Sorry, a failed attempt at humor. As you are aware, Randolph, being fifty, retired a few weeks ago from the department. Being a police officer in a big city can wear on you, and I imagine he wants a bit of a slower pace. In his younger days he was a real go-getter, but he has slowed down over the past few years. He shouldn't have any trouble looking after a small town."

"Thanks for your time," Mike said.

"Certainly. And you needn't worry about his adjoining a bottle of Scotch every day. That rarely interferes with his duties."

The council members traded glances.

"Thanks again, Chief," Mike said as he hung up the phone.

Jessie looked at Mike and asked, "Do we want a heavy drinker as police chief?"

The council members simultaneously cachinnated.

After the laughter abated, Mike said, "I'll call Mr. Blane and tell him he's got the job. Only in California would they describe a man who drinks too much as 'adjoining a bottle.'"

The phone rang in Randolph's apartment in Los Angeles.

"Hello?"

"Randolph, Mike Smith here. I wanted to let you know you've got the job."

"That's fine. I'd like to make one request, if I may."

"Go ahead."

"I'd prefer to wear civilian clothes, no uniform."

"No problem. Some chiefs in the past didn't don a uniform. I can't see anyone objecting."

"I'll leave in a day or so and be in Bane next Monday."

"Good. See you then. Bye."

Randolph pulled out two new suitcases. He wanted to start afresh and take as little as possible. He had purchased two new pairs of jeans, several plaid flannel shirts, a heavy jacket, underwear, and pajamas. He took an eight-by-ten picture off the shelf.

"Sorry, Siobhan. It's been twenty years." He put the picture and frame with the items he would be taking to Goodwill. He told his landlady he was leaving the furniture, that she was welcome to it. The next morning he headed to his new job.

After Mike had called Randolph, he called Amaryllis.

"Hello?"

"Amaryllis, the council all agreed, and we hired the new chief. He'll be here next Monday. After he gets settled in, we're going to have the matter at hand taken care of."

There was silence.

"Amaryllis, you there?"

"Yes, but I don't know what you're expecting from me."

"Ah . . . well . . . I thought you should know."

"Fine, you told me." Amaryllis hung up.

Mike pulled the phone away from his face, looked at it, and shrugged.

Amaryllis walked over to her bureau and pulled out her picture of Travis when he was sixteen. They had known for years that they would marry. Then a few weeks after this picture was taken, he died. Why had she been dreaming about him so much lately? Why was she so edgy? Was she tired of her job, her employer? It was because of Travis— sort of—that she became a psychiatrist. One of Travis's older brothers was diagnosed as schizophrenic. In sessions with the psychiatrist, Travis's mother was told it was her fault her son was schizophrenic, that she had been a bad mother. A common diagnosis at the time: the mother's fault. A few months later the mother died in her sleep. No cause, her heart just stopped. And several months after that, Travis died the same way. No cause, in his sleep. Both Travis and Amaryllis knew that Travis's mother was tormented with guilt, and then Travis with sadness. Amaryllis prayed about the best way to help people, and she became a psychiatrist.

When she was studying psychiatry, she worked with a team of psychiatrists that produced evidence that schizophrenia was biological—not the mother's fault.

Randolph found a small house to rent a few miles outside of Bane. He'd been in town for less than three weeks. The only thing that identified him as chief was a badge—in his pocket. On the way to work he stopped at the Jiffy Mart on the town outskirts for a bottle of Scotch—as usual. After looking around the mart, he approached the register where the owner was standing. He'd met Mr. Baker a few days earlier at the meet and greet, but this was the first time he had seen him in the Jiffy Mart. Normally Renee was at the register.

"Mr. Baker, good morning. Ah . . . where's the liquor?"

"Liquor?"

"Yes. I'm looking for a bottle of Scotch."

"Stopped selling liquor, Chief."

"Oh, why is that?"

"Can I be frank?"

"Always."

"I decided to stop selling it when I heard you adjoin a bottle of Scotch every day. I don't believe the chief of police should be a heavy drinker. And Renee said you come in almost every day and pick up a bottle of Scotch."

Randolph nodded and smiled. *Small town*, he thought.

"I see. How's business, without the alcohol sales?"

"Well, it's only been a couple of days, but pretty bad. I'll probably have to let Renee go, or at least cut back her hours and man the register myself, like today."

Randolph liked Renee, a young woman only two years out of high school who graduated at the top of her class. Overall one of the most pleasant people he'd met. If he wasn't careful, they could get into a thirty-minute conversation about any number of people: Aristotle, Cicero, Aspasia, John Locke, Damaris Masham.

"I tell you what, Mr. Baker. If you start selling alcohol again, I promise I'll never buy any."

"You promise? Even Scotch?"

"Yes, even Scotch."

"Thank goodness."

"You're welcome." Randolph headed to the office.

On a Saturday several weeks later, Randolph walked into the town library. He wanted to get an idea who the big readers were. In a small town, the librarians usually knew the back stories. Plus, he wanted to check out a book.

He walked over to the librarian, Mrs. Davis, and asked, "Can I see the records of your customers?"

"You mean who's checked out books?"

"Forsooth."

Randolph had met Mrs. Davis at the meet and greet and learned they were both fond of archaic words. Mrs. Davis would normally have asked for a warrant, but their prior conversation had been delightful.

"Certes. Let's go to my office, and I'll pull up the files on the computer."

After the files were accessed, Randolph sat down, and Mrs. Davis showed him different ways to sort the information. Randolph sorted by who checked out the most books.

"Hardy Bruckner; it looks as if he's your best customer?"

"Yes. Eighty years old, and he often comes in if he's not fishing on that small pier at the north end of town near his house. Loves to read, as you see. A nice man. If you need to know any history of the town or folks, he's a gold mine."

"Thanks, Mrs. Davis, that's all I need."

"You sure? You didn't stay long."

"Long enough to find a gold mine."

Mrs. Davis chuckled. "That's true. And please, call me Gwen."

"Thanks, Gwen. I'm going to look around for a book or two."

"By all means."

The pair returned to the main part of the library.

Randolph sat down at one of the tables and pulled out his notebook, setting it on the table. The next book on his list not crossed off was *Middlemarch*. It was a thicker book than those he usually read—he would often get bored if the book was too long—but it was a must-read, or so *they* said. Ah, the proverbial *they*. His eyes took in the next few books on the list, and he looked up. A young woman, the prettiest woman he'd seen since moving to Bane, had entered the library. She looked to be in her late thirties, five foot nine and 130 pounds, with red hair that fell just below her shoulders. Her jeans were well-fitting, as was her pullover wool top that went up her lower neck. The only jewelry she wore was a crucifix around her neck, resting on the wool at her cleavage. She froze at the sight of Randolph and then regained her composure and walked over to Gwen.

The library was small with waist-high shelves, and Randolph could see virtually the entire library from his vantage point. The woman and Gwen exchanged a few words as they glanced at Randolph. Then the woman spent a few minutes looking at some books before she held one tightly. Randolph carefully watched the woman, as if he couldn't avert his eyes from her. Suddenly she marched right up to Randolph's table and put her book down.

"Hello," she said to Randolph, giving him a hard stare.

"Hello yourself." Expect the unexpected—a motto of his.

"I noticed you checking me out. You like what you see?" the woman asked.

"Forsooth."

"What do you like best?" The woman proceeded to stand in various poses and then put both hands on the back of her neck and flipped out her hair, something she hadn't done in years with Travis.

"Your book selection," Randolph replied.

"Uh-huh . . . no doubt," she said as she frowned and picked up her book.

"The first book you looked at, *Aristotle's Way* by Edith Hall, one of my favorites. Then *A Discourse on Natural Religion* by David Hume. A bit of a hard read, since it was written over three hundred years ago and not a book I would expect someone wearing a crucifix to have high on their list. Finally *Middlemarch*, the next book on my reading list. It appears you've checked it out. I guess I'll have to wait to read it unless I drive to the Barnes & Noble in Augusta and buy it."

The bedazzled woman sat down across from Randolph.

Randolph's notebook was lying open on the table. He turned it around and slid it to the woman.

She looked down at the list.

"Well, you certainly are a surprise, Chief. In more ways than one." The woman had not been at the meet and greet.

"You know who I am?"

"Small town. I asked Gwen about you when I came in. I don't live here. I live and work in the next town over, but I'm in Bane on occasion."

"And you hear all the town news?"

"Yes. People are inclined to tell me things."

"Why is that?"

"Maybe it's because I am a psychiatrist."

"Really?"

"I have a few clients in Bane. And at times I would consult with the prior chief on a case."

"Actually I'm going to be interviewing psychiatrists in the area; I'm looking for someone who can help me occasionally." Everybody lies, ever and anon.

"Is that so?" The woman's eyebrows went up.

"I'd like to ask you out to dinner next Thursday night."

"Well, if you'd like to, maybe you should."

"Will you have dinner with me? Assuming your husband doesn't mind."

"No husband. And yes, I'll have dinner with you."

"What time should I pick you up?"

"I'll meet you at the Barbay downtown at six."

"Okay."

The woman stood up.

Randolph stood. "I don't know your name."

"No, you don't. Amaryllis Ware."

The pair shook hands, and Amaryllis was on her way.

As she walked to her car, Amaryllis smiled and thought, *My God*. She knew no one in town would gossip about her to the chief. They wouldn't dare.

After checking out his book, Randolph crossed the street to the town park. It was in the center of town and the size of a city block. Trees were scattered throughout except for the park's center, which was grass. Other than picnic tables, trees, and grass, there was naught. This was where the meet and greet was held after he arrived. He had been introduced to one of the trees—Malvern, the hanging tree. It was three hundred or so years old and bore a historical marker. The marker reflected the approximate age of the tree and the fact that three people who were convicted as witches were hanged from it.

Randolph sat at one of the picnic tables and opened his book. After reading for a bit, he headed to the small pier where Hardy Bruckner was known to fish. Randolph parked not far from the pier, grabbed his fishing rod and folding chair from the trunk, and headed to the pier. The pier was short and jutted out into a narrow river. It wasn't a popular place, as only one person was fishing. Most folks fished off the pier that jutted into the Atlantic on the other side of town.

A man sat in a chair fishing. Randolph approached and set his own chair down a few feet from the man.

"Afternoon," Randolph said.

"Afternoon, Chief," the man said.

"You know who I am?"

"Small town. I'm Hardy Bruckner," the man said and held out his hand.

Randolph shook his hand and got his rod ready to fish. It took no coaxing for Hardy to begin telling his life history with bits of Bane's history mixed in. He had been a deckhand on one of the smaller fishing trawlers for most of his life. At a certain point Randolph asked if the townsfolk were talking about him.

"Yep, folks wondering why the town council hired you, considering you're a heavy drinking man."

"And what conclusion have they reached?"

"Think maybe the council is up to no good and that you won't notice, being a drinking man."

"I understand the council members didn't know each other before they ran for council."

"They knew each other very well, but that was a lot of years ago, and they haven't mingled for the past sixty years."

"Oh, so they were friends when they were kids?"

"Yep. The four of them and a boy named Tony who lives in Boston now. They were incorrigible. When they were five or so, they straightened up and stopped having anything to do with each other."

"Why was that?"

"Well, most folks don't know it, but this is what happened . . . ."

Hardy told Randolph the whole story.

"That's horrible, but it doesn't indicate what they might be up to."

"Well, there's the one constant reminder. All four, not counting Tony, have been Amaryllis's patients for years and another psychiatrist before her. But Tony, poor kid, no one ever tried to help him, and look how he turned out."

The conversation drifted to other things.

It was Wednesday night at nine, and the last citizen walked out of the monthly town council meeting. Randolph, standing in the back of the room, waved to the four council members, Mike, Jessie, Tucker, and Sam, and headed home.

"Gosh, I haven't officially closed the meeting," Mike said. "And everyone has left."

"That's a shame, considering we have one more item of business we need to address," Jessie said. All the council members smiled.

"Yes, it's about you-know-what," Tucker said, and they all nodded.

"Can we help it if everyone left before I closed the meeting? Still, we're not in violation of the open-meetings law if we conduct business," Mike said.

"Good, because we've waited long enough," Sam said.

"Too long," Tucker replied. "We'll have to find someone from Boston to do it. We can't take the chance of someone here finding out."

"Tony will do it," Mike said.

"You know that?" Sam asked.

"Think about it," Mike replied.

The other three council members nodded.

"Tony runs one of the mob families in Boston. He'll be able to get people to do it—people who will keep their mouths shut," Mike said. "I'll call him, and we'll go down to Boston and work out the details."

"I don't think we want the details," Sam said. "The less we know, the better."

The other three nodded.

"I'll go ahead and write what we agree to in the minutes, in couched terms of course, so we can at least avoid any legal trouble on account of the open-meetings law."

The next day Mike called Tony to set up a meeting. What Mike didn't know was that he made their lunch appointment at the most popular restaurant in Boston, a restaurant frequented by newspaper photographers.

Randolph pulled into the Jiffy Mart on the edge of town as he did every day on his way to the office.

"Good morning, Renee," he said as he walked in.

"Morning, Chief," she replied. "Oh, by the way, I agree with you, *The Walking Drum* by Louis L'Amour is very good. I finished it last night. And I thought he had only written cowboy novels."

"Glad you enjoyed it."

"You and Amaryllis give me the best reading suggestions."

"I'll look over my list tonight; give you another recommendation tomorrow."

Randolph ambled down one of the aisles and picked up a bottle of Scotch. He was looking at the bottle when Renee walked up behind him and asked, "Was it your father and brother who were alcoholics?"

Randolph turned around. "What?"

"Well, everybody in town—except me—believes you're an alcoholic after that conversation the town council had with the chief in LA. That your 'adjoining a bottle of Scotch every day' didn't interfere with your work. But you come in here well-nigh every day and pick up a bottle of Scotch, in effect adjoining a bottle of Scotch. Then you look at it and put it back. I surmise that you're a teetotaler. If it was only your father who was an alcoholic, you wouldn't need to look at a bottle of Scotch every day. But you do it because your brother drinks. And when someone asks your brother why he's an alcoholic, I aver he says, 'My father was an alcoholic, so what do you expect?' But if someone asked you why you don't drink, you say the same thing, 'My father was an alcoholic, so what do you expect?' You reinforce your belief that humans have free will; that our decisions are not determined solely by our genes, by our environment, by the amniotic fluid that surrounded us before birth."

Randolph took in Renee more carefully than he had before

and said, "I've heard that you were valedictorian when you graduated two years ago."

"I was."

"Would you be interested in becoming a police officer?"

"What? Why?"

"Did you deduce all of that on your own?"

"Yes, and I told Mr. Baker about it."

"What did he think?"

"He said, 'You think so?' I'm pretty sure he believes it now."

"Having a sixth sense is helpful in police work. Has anyone told you that you have a sixth sense?

"Amaryllis . . . she said I should become a psychiatrist."

"That's not a bad idea either."

"You like her, Amaryllis, don't you? You two talking in the library caused quite a stir."

"Yes, I do. What are people saying about Amaryllis and me?"

"Nothing."

"Nothing . . . remarkable."

"People gossip about you, but not Amaryllis."

"Because she's a psychiatrist?"

"Yeah . . . no doubt." Renee smiled and walked back to the register.

It was Thursday at six, and Randolph walked into the Barbay. Amaryllis was seated at a table toward the back, and he sat down across from her.

"Good evening, Amaryllis. Still wearing your library outfit, I see."

"You know how to make a girl feel special."

"Maybe that's why I've never been married."

"Never?"

"Engaged once; Siobhan Merrimack . . . she was a clarinet-ist for the Los Angeles Symphony."

"Was?"

"She died."

"Sorry. You have a picture of her?"

Randolph shook his head.

"About my outfit: in my calling it is more or less required to keep things simple."

"Don't want to be off-putting to your patients. Makes sense."

Amaryllis passed Randolph a menu, and they ordered.

"I understand you're a heavy drinker," Amaryllis said.

"That's my understanding too," Randolph said, trying to be cute but realizing Amaryllis might mistake it for an ac-knowledgment. "What makes you ask?"

"I've been successful in helping alcoholics."

"The next time you encounter Renee, ask her about my so-called drinking problem. She's got an excellent perspective on it."

"Renee at the Jiffy Mart?" Amaryllis asked.

"Yes. By the way, what can you tell me about the town council? I'm wondering why they hired a police chief who picks up a bottle of Scotch every day."

"You want facts or gossip?"

"Facts; gossip, if it helps."

"They're all new to politics. First time any of them ran for office."

"Any idea why they ran for office now?"

"Well, they all recently retired."

"Anything else?"

"No."

There was an awkward silence and then Randolph said, "Ah . . . all four . . . clients of yours, perchance?"

More silence.

"Let's not spoil the evening," Amaryllis said.

"Quite right."

The remaining conversation was pleasant for both parties, and as they stood outside to say goodbye for the night, Randolph merely held out his hand to shake. "This has been a pleasant evening, Amaryllis. How about we do this every Thursday night?"

"I'd like that," she replied. They shook hands and were on their way.

Amaryllis and Randolph stood a foot apart. She closed the gap and kissed him passionately. Before he knew it, he was watching the back of her naked body walking into his bedroom.

"Randolph, Randolph," called Amaryllis.

Randolph stirred. Opening his eyes, he looked at the other side of his rumpled king-sized bed and sat up.

"Randolph, you awake?"

Randolph shot up out of bed. "Jeez!" he said, in a state of confusion.

"Sorry for waking you," Amaryllis said as she knocked on the bedroom window again.

Randolph opened the curtains to find Amaryllis standing in his yard.

"I had a good time last night at dinner. Sorry to wake you, but I finished *Middlemarch* in bed last night, so I came over and put it on your porch. It looks as if it will rain, and I didn't want the book to get wet. I'm late for an appointment: I'll talk to you later." She turned and left.

"Good gracious," he said as he plopped on the bed trying to remember if there was more to his dream.

The next day Randolph stopped at the Jiffy Mart on his way to work and saw Mr. Baker at the register.

"Morning, Chief," Mr. Baker said as Randolph walked in.

"Morning."

"Here to pick up a bottle of Scotch?"

"You know it."

After replacing the bottle of Scotch, Randolph approached the register. There in the newspaper rack was a Boston paper with a front-page picture of the members of Bane's town council and another man having lunch. Randolph picked up the paper.

"Picture got your attention, did it?" Mr. Baker said.

"Yeah."

"This will certainly get people in town chin-wagging."

"Why's that?"

"According to the paper, the fifth man in the picture is a suspected mob boss. Supposedly he'll take care of someone for the right price."

"Interesting."

"Sam was in here earlier, and I asked him about it."

"What did he say?"

"Said the restaurant was crowded, and they had to let someone use the seat."

"You believe him?"

"To tell the truth, Chief—no."

"Why?"

"He turned crimson when he saw the picture."

"Are these all the papers you've got?"

"That's it; what's in the rack."

Randolph picked up all the papers and put them on the counter, wondering why Sam hadn't bought all of them.

"You're buying all of them?"

"Yep."

"Okay."

"Thanks. See you later," Randolph said.

On the way to the office, Randolph got a call on the radio. "Go ahead," he said.

"Chief, you need to head over to the city park. A crime has been committed," the dispatcher said.

As Randolph was driving through the park, he saw the problem, pulled to the curb, and joined Deputy Jenkins.

"Well, Chief, I guess we have a murder on our hands, after a fashion," Jenkins said.

"I see," Randolph said. "They weren't taking any chances. It looks as if they did a complete job."

"Yep. Malvern's gone, with no trace other than a bunch of twigs from Malvern lying in the street and sidewalk. A semi must have been parked over there. They must have used a crane and pulled Malvern right out of the ground—roots and all."

"Is the district attorney available? I want to find out what laws have been broken."

"He's on vacation, Chief. But I'm sure he's going to want the maximum penalty. After all, he's head of the Bane Historical Association," Jenkins replied.

Randolph was thinking that the four members of the Bane

Town Council had committed the crime or had at least ordered it. He thought it would be best to confirm his suspicions by talking to Amaryllis, as they were her patients.

Randolph pulled up to the steps at the address he'd been given for Amaryllis's place of employment and looked up at the imposing building. It couldn't be the right place. He walked down the driveway to the street and looked at the number on the stone pillar, comparing it to the number on his notepad. Same number.

He walked back up the driveway and entered a large hall with high ceilings. He approached a desk off to the side of a large winding staircase that curved upward to the second floor, but no one was at the desk. There were huge doors to the left and right of the stairs; he took the stairs. On the second floor a woman came out of one of the rooms, closed the door, and came toward him.

Randolph pulled out his badge. "Excuse me."

"Yes, can I help you?"

"I'm looking for Amaryllis Ware. Official business."

"Ah, you must be Randolph," the woman said as she held out her hand. "Small towns. Follow me." After a short walk the woman pointed to a door. "That's her office. Just knock and walk right in."

Randolph watched the woman walk away. He turned a few steps to the door, knocked, and walked in.

Amaryllis was sitting at a large desk and looked up.

"Yes . . . oh, Randolph. This is a surprise."

"You're not nearly as surprised as I am."

"I was going to tell you when the time was right."

"Renee didn't tell me where you worked, just the address. Now I know why she hemmed and hawed so."

"I guess this is business?"

"Yes." Randolph laid a copy of the Boston paper on the desk and pointed to the photograph. "Five men who sixty years ago were hellraising five-year-old boys and this man," Randolph said, pointing at Tony. "His father and one of the other boys' fathers—I don't know who—took the boys to Malvern one night after dark. Over one of the branches were five nooses with a chair under each noose. The boys were stood on a chair and a noose was put around their necks. They were told that because they were bad, they would be hanged just like the witches hundreds of years ago. The boys cried and soiled their clothes. After Tony's father recited their sins, he made as if he was going to kick away the chairs. Instead he laughed and walked away. The other man took down the boys and told them if they continued to be bad, they would be hanged. The boys stopped being bad and stopped playing together. I understand why they would want to get rid of Malvern, but they broke the law. I need you to confirm that it was the council members who had this done."

"My records are confidential. Besides, it's only a tree."

"I don't make the law."

"You want a sip of water?"

"Sure."

Amaryllis picked up a glass off her desk and handed it to Randolph, who took a few sips.

"You going to have a glass?" Randolph asked.

"That is my glass." She took the glass, took a sip, and put it back on the desk. "Let's sit on the sofa."

Randolph walked over to a long leather sofa and sat down. Amaryllis sat beside him.

"Now I know why people in Bane don't gossip about you. I thought it was because you're a psychiatrist."

"And what do you think now?"

"I think it's because . . . well—"

"Because I'm an abbess; a nun who runs a convent."

Randolph nodded.

"You're probably right. Either they're being considerate or they're afraid of Hell. But let's get back to why you're here. The town council did not break the law. Normally it's against the law to destroy a historical site, but in this case it's not. The law, item 27(f) of section 87(b) allows a mayor or town council to remove a historic site. And one of the definitions of *remove* is to eliminate." As Amaryllis spoke, she patted Randolph's leg softly several times, and her hand stayed on his leg.

"Are you allowed to do that?" Randolph asked, looking at her hand on his leg.

Amaryllis removed her hand from his leg, placed it behind his head, pulled him toward her, and gave him a passionate kiss.

When it ended Randolph said, "I'm pretty sure nuns aren't allowed to do that!"

"I'll have to go to confession. Then I'll do my penance."

"What if the priest is a tattletale and tells the Pope?"

"He's not allowed to."

"What is the name of your order?"

"The Sisters of Heloise."

Randolph was taken aback. His shoulders jerked back slightly, and his eyes narrowed. He and Amaryllis gazed into each other's eyes, and then they both burst out laughing.

"You're such a tease," Randolph said.

"Yes, I am." Amaryllis stood up and went behind her desk.

Randolph walked to the desk as well, standing across from Amaryllis. "Does this mean our Thursday night dates . . . dinners . . . are over?"

"Not at all."

"What about that?" Randolph said, nodding at the sofa.

"What about what?"

"You know . . . the kiss."

"There will be no more kissing."

Randolph nodded, disappointed.

Amaryllis continued, "Unless you ask me to marry you. I'll say yes, resign, and I'll kiss you like that every day. Maybe more than once a day."

The biggest grin he'd ever had was plastered on Randolph's face. "See you Thursday," he said as he was leaving the office. "Oh, you might want to type your resignation letter; you'll be turning it in on Friday morning."

That evening as Randolph sat in his fireside rocker listening to Brahms, he reflected on his encounter with Amaryllis earlier that day. He stood up, walked to the bedroom, and picked up his wallet before heading back to the rocker. He opened the wallet and pulled out his picture of Siobhan. It could have been a picture of Amaryllis. It's best she never know what Siobhan looked like, he thought, throwing it into the fireplace.

In her room after her prayers that evening, Amaryllis put on Vivaldi. She walked to her bureau, opened the top drawer, and pulled out a picture of Travis at sixteen. The spitting image of Randolph stared back at her. She thought it best that Randolph never know what Travis looked like. She ripped the picture into little pieces.

A thousand miles away at the University of . . . well, the name doesn't matter, a conversation was taking place.

"Dwight, you think there's something to this?" Professor Simon asked.

"There are strong indications that it's true, but we can't prove it with the data we have."

"I don't even know how you could design an experiment to prove this."

"That's the problem. There are just too many variables you'd need to control, monitor, and measure, that you can't."

"Still, I'm intrigued with the theory that who you fall in love with is triggered by the proportions and attributes of a person's face. That at some point when you're growing up, it could be at one year old, two years old, or four years old, a face strikes your brain in such a way that it creates an imprint you're not even aware of in the part of the brain that becomes active when your hormones kick in. Then when you're older and you see a face that has those proportions and attributes, you fall in love. I wish we could test this."

"But then again, those people who don't believe in free will, will love this. And I'm not sure that not believing in free will is a good thing."

"You may be right."

The End

7

I Have to Do What?

As usual Judge Cutler and his wife, Burgundy, were having supper in their dining room.

"What time are your visitors arriving?" Burgundy asked.

"At eight o'clock."

"And they're police?"

"That's my impression."

"What do they want?"

"Normal police stuff, I guess. They were a bit vague."

"I'll be at that lecture at Stanford Law. Y'all have fun. Oh, by the way. . ."

"Yes?"

"Your latest ruling is wrong."

Judge Cutler peered up and said, "Which ruling?"

"The executive branch versus congressional representatives on whether the House of Representatives must raise the debt ceiling for the government to pay its bills."

"What? The Constitution gives Congress the power to collect taxes and spend money—no ifs, ands, or buts."

"True, but it gives Congress no right to ignore debts Congress already incurred or promised. You didn't review the

Fourteenth Amendment, did you? 'The validity of the public debt of the United States . . . shall not be questioned.' You don't get a do-over if debts have been incurred or promised. You must pay them notwithstanding. This debt ceiling nonsense that started in 1917 is just sound and fury, signifying nothing." Burgundy stood and strode over to the shelf of law books. She pulled down three and placed them on the table for her husband. "Here. I've marked three different items you need to review. But not to worry; your ruling will be overturned on appeal." Burgundy started clearing the table.

Dang, thought Judge Cutler. If he weren't retiring at the end of the week, he would have needed to hire a new law clerk. Normally Judge Cutler would follow Burgundy into the kitchen and dry the dishes as she washed, but he was so busy reading that he didn't notice that she had dried the dishes, changed into a smart outfit, and left for the lecture. A short time later, his guests arrived. After some pleasantries, the agents explained why they were there. Judge Cutler was gobsmacked at their offer.

"Yes, Judge Cutler, we're serious. The job is yours if you want it," Agent Corner said.

"But . . . well . . . I've never done this kind of work. I'm a judge, and you want me to head up the—"

"Yes sir, we do. We've found that judges are good at . . . well . . . judging things, things like truth and lies. Lots of practice. We've examined the records of thousands of judges, and you came out on the tippy top."

"You know I've always been interested in the spy game."

"We know. We have a list of all the books you've ever bought or checked out of the library. You got extra credit for that—the books you read."

"Gee, I might find the work very interesting. Tell me,

would I have access to all the files? I mean all the historical stuff: Oswald, Bay of Pigs, and such?"

Agent Corner and Agent Sample glanced at each other.

"I don't see why not, but we've never had anyone ask afore," replied Agent Corner.

"This could work out nicely. I've already submitted my retirement paperwork."

"Yes, we know."

"I assume you've done a complete background check hitherto."

"Of course."

"How long do I have to think about it?"

"Twenty-four hours."

"That's all?"

"We've found that people who take longer never pan out."

"I see," the judge said, deep in thought while drumming his fingers on his desk. "Can I take my desk with me?"

The two agents eyeballed each other.

"I don't think that—"

"It's just that it used to belong to Napoleon."

"We can make an exception. But it will have to pass a security clearance, and sometimes French things don't pass. But then again, at least it's not an English desk. The English are still on the outs because of Philby."

"Gentlemen, I will expect you back tomorrow and give you my decision. But I have to say I'm inclined to take it."

"Excellent."

The two agents stood, started toward the door, and then turned back.

"Judge Cutler, there is one more minor requirement for the position."

"Yes? What is it?"

"You have to divorce your wife."

"*I have to do what?* Surely you're kidding."

"No sir. And you'll have to marry someone else."

"Goodness! I guess I will have to think about it."

"And Judge Cutler, we have the new wife picked out. This is her bio," Agent Corner said as he handed the judge a sheet of paper.

The judge perused it. "Uh . . . you don't have someone else available?"

"Someone else?"

"Someone . . . ah . . . perchance a bit younger. This woman is forty-eight."

Agent Corner and Agent Sample glanced at each other.

Agent Corner responded, "No one. This agent's mother is an agent, her father is an agent, her sister is an agent, and her brother is an agent. Most of your socializing, outings, and the like will be with them. Like having your own security detail. Here's her photo, sir. Maybe that will help."

"Whoa . . . and she's forty-eight?" Judge Cutler said in a high-pitched squeal.

"Yes. And the wedding must be simple, private—a justice of the peace and a couple of witnesses."

"OK. I'm still inclined to accept the position. See you fellows tomorrow."

As the agents drove away, Agent Sample said, "That was cute about the family members being agents too."

"I thought so," replied Agent Corner.

The following afternoon, Judge Cutler was rocking on the porch when Burgundy got home.

"What're you doing out here?" Burgundy asked.

"Enjoying the outdoors. I'll be in soon."

"OK." Burgundy went into the house.

Anon, Agents Corner and Sample drove into the driveway.

Judge Cutler rushed to the car before the agents even opened their doors.

"I agree to take the job and head up the agency," Judge Cutler said. "What happens now?"

"Here are the divorce papers your wife needs to sign. You won't have a problem getting her to sign, will you?"

"Nah. I'm always pulling pranks. She'll think that's what it is, a prank. Besides, I've bought her something; she'll be distracted. And I can get another judge to approve the divorce documents tomorrow."

"Fine. We'll meet you tomorrow in your chamber at four thirty and go over the remaining details. Should be able to have you remarried by the weekend and your new office set up next week too. Your office will be in the Garner Building downtown."

"My office isn't at Langley?"

"It will be, but the Langley building is being remodeled. Probably another month or two."

"OK. Tomorrow then."

Agents Corner and Sample drove away.

After the judge and his wife ate supper and washed and put away the dishes, Judge Cutler and Burgundy were reading in the den.

"Burgundy, I bought you a present."

"Oh," Burgundy said as she glanced around the room for something new.

"I know how much you enjoy your monthly getaways to Acapulco, so I bought you that Airbnb where you like to stay. It's yours."

"What? Really?"

"Yep. Hired a handyman and cleaning crew to spruce it up. Here are their numbers. You can call and arrange whatever work you want to be done."

"That's fantastic; I love that place."

"I know. Oh yeah, here's something I need you to sign." Judge Cutler handed Burgundy the divorce decree, turning to the page she needed to sign.

"What's this?"

"A divorce decree. I'm going to have a little fun with—"

"Sure, here you go," said Burgundy as she signed the document and handed it back to her husband.

"Ah . . . thanks."

"No problem. I was going to divorce you anyway." Burgundy said, laughing.

Judge Cutler laughed too, albeit hesitantly.

Three weeks later Burgundy was sitting under a beach umbrella by the pool at a hotel in Acapulco. Handymen and cleaners were at her house preparing it for her to move into the day after next.

A man walked around the pool and sat in the lounge chair beside Burgundy. He was tall, handsome, and tanned. He looked as if he worked out and appeared to be thirty-eight or so.

"What are you doing here, Tony?" Burgundy asked.

"Mr. Harper sent me. Got one more bill for you to take care of."

"Oh?"

Tony handed Burgundy an itemized summary with the final amount due. After a minute Tony asked, "Something wrong?"

"No, nothing. I was just wondering. Could we get my husband—ex-husband—to make the final payment?"

They both chuckled.

"It looks like Corner and Sample were a bargain," Burgundy noted.

"Out-of-work actors; the town is full of them. They were glad to do it for pennies on the dollar. Said they had fun with Judge Cutler."

"I've got an idea. Work up an invoice for my remaining balance, a bill for moving Napoleon's desk to my ex-husband's new office, and send it to him."

They both burst out laughing again.

"I like it. I'll do it. Mr. Harper will think it's swell. How did you come to hire his firm for this job?"

"Known him since middle school. We used to watch *Perry Mason* together. I knew he'd become a detective, as he always admired Paul Drake more than Perry Mason."

"And this will do it? Get you what you want?"

"Yep, my dad is in ill health, in a coma, and will be gone in a day or two. Found out in his will that he was leaving half of everything—and the lake house—to my husband. But everything goes to me if we're divorced and he remarries."

"Good show."

"What will happen to the woman my husband married?"

"She'll disappear, long-term covert assignment in Russia. Didn't even have time to consummate the marriage. Soon all his contacts will disappear. If he looks hard enough, he'll find that the office he was using was rented by a front company, untraceable. And, of course, no one at Langley will know anything about it."

"Maybe I could remarry him after a bit. He wasn't a bad sort."

Tony shrugged.

"But then again, Tony, you're not wearing a ring, and I'm about to be a rich woman."

At the same time in Hollywood, California, Mr. Cutler was answering the knock on his office door in the Garner building. His office didn't have a reception area, which was just as well, as he didn't have a receptionist.

"Ah, Mr. Harper, please come in. Have a seat."

Mr. Cutler returned to his desk that once belonged to Napoleon and sat down.

"Here's the report on your situation and your itemized bill."

Mr. Cutler took the report—a page and a half—and read it.

"So, all this—?" Mr. Cutler waved his hand around the office.

"Is phony, yes," replied Mr. Harper.

"Oh, Burgundy," Mr. Cutler said as he sighed. "What a waste! It explains why I've had almost nothing to do the past few weeks." He pulled out his checkbook to pay the bill.

"You're not going to swear, throw things, the typical reaction when a husband discovers something like this?"

"No, Mr. Harper. Why would I? Burgundy was a fine wife for forty years. It's my fault for being gullible, selfish, and untoward. I can live fine on my pension. And the lake house is three hours away; I'd never use it. And as far as the will goes, I knew my father-in-law was leaving me half. That's why I got him to change it and leave everything to Burgundy. He left the old will lying around his house before he shredded it. She must have seen it."

"What are you going to do now?"

"A vacation mayhap. I understand Acapulco is nice this time of year. Perhaps I'll run into someone looking for a husband, or at least a friend."

The End

Printed in the USA
CPSIA information can be obtained
at www.ICGtesting.com
JSHW080232150824
68020JS00001B/106